NAMING THE

WINDS

NAMING THE WINDS

A HIGH PLAINS
APPRENTICESHIP

CAROLINE MARWITZ

HIGH PLAINS PRESS

BIO
MARWITZ

FIRST PRINTING

10 9 8 7 6 5 4 3 2 1

AUTHOR'S NOTE:

The events in this book are as I remember them. In a few
instances names outside the family have been changed.

Library of Congress Cataloging-in-Publication Data

Marwitz, Caroline

Naming the winds : a high plains apprenticeship /
Caroline Marwitz.

p.cm.

ISBN 0-931271-57-6 (alk. paper)

1. Marwitz, Caroline

2. Laramie (Wyo.)--Biography.

I. Title.

CT275.M4612A3 2000

978.7'1903'092--dc21

[B]   00-057566

HIGH PLAINS PRESS

539 CASSA ROAD

GLENDO, WYOMING 82213

WWW.HIGHPLAINSPRESS.COM

ORDERS: 1-800-552-7819

To Curt

*Whose birthday wish every year for
twenty years has been the same one.
Thank you.*

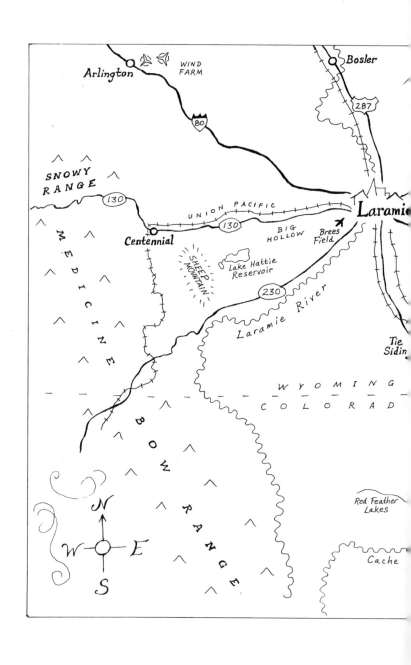

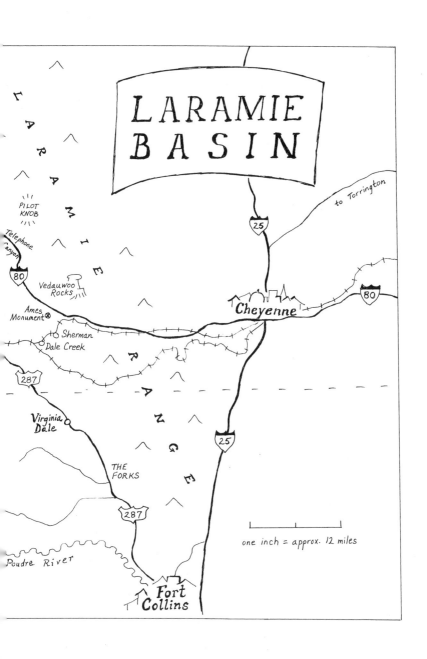

LARAMIE BASIN

one inch = approx. 12 miles

My heartfelt gratitude goes to Nancy Curtis and Mindy Keskinen, without whom this book would not exist. Any errors or ambiguities of explanation regarding scientific or historic fact are my own.

I am also grateful to the many others who kept me going, whether they knew it or not: Thank you for asking me how the writing was going; thank you for giving advice; thank you for reading the manuscript; thank you for answering my questions; thank you for loaning me a computer; thank you for telling me, "Don't give up, Carol." Thank you, all of you.

Contents

Grass Comb Wind: *Midsummer* 11

Silk Wind: *End of summer,
beginning of autumn* 31

Rattlesnake Wind: *Full autumn* 47

Moth Tongue Wind: *Late autumn* 57

White Locust Wind: *Early winter* 77

Coyote Wind: *Winter* 93

Skipping Stone Wind: *Winter suspended* 105

Chinook Wind: *Deep winter* 129

Feather Merchant Wind: *False spring* 143

Thunder Hoof Wind: *Spring* 159

Little Verdigris Wind: *Late spring,
hesitant beginning of summer* 175

Fire Eyes Wind: *Early summer* 195

Speckled Rising Wind: *Summer* 211

GRASS COMB WIND

Midsummer

ᴄᴏ   THERE ONCE WAS an old woman who lived in the eye of the wind. Breezes swirled leaves in whirlwinds down her street and gales scoured the prairie, ripping the shutters off her neighbor's house, but her yard and house were unscathed. Her house was a rosy sandstone fortress that budged not an inch under the raking teeth of the Wyoming wind, though year by year its stony walls lost grain after grain of pale pink sand. The stone was the pink-orange color of sunset, quarried from the hills east of Laramie. The woman and her husband had built the house long ago when they were young.

A cedar fence around the stone house helped keep the wind from rattling the lace-curtained windows. The intense rains of summer afternoons soaked the fence and darkened it to a deep golden brown. Afterwards, steam rose from the wood in the sudden warmth of the sunlight and the smell of a cedar forest wafted across the prairie.

Between house and fence stood a grove of trees where several old female cottonwoods grew. Three stories high, they couldn't hide from the wind. How those trees roared sometimes, as the wind moved through their branches. It was almost as if the branches themselves created the wind, fanning small breezes to gale strength. Old gray goddesses of leaf and bark, each had a name, I learned later: Nina, Erin, and Anne.

I loved the house and the trees even before I met the old woman, their owner. I used to ride past on my bike, stop and prop it against the fence, and peer between the cedar planks at the old-fashioned house with its grove and gardens. I'd try to imagine what it would be like to live there, encompassed by the stone walls, to sit in the deep-set windowsills and watch the wind as it handled every twig of those huge trees.

When I remember my childhood in Wyoming, this is what I see: a grassy blanket of summer green stretching for miles between walls of blue mountains, the wind blowing—always the wind—and the woman who owned that house. As the years go by, the memory of her becomes mixed with the memory of my grandma's strong hands kneading flour into pota-to bread dough, my mother's dark eyes flashing indig-nantly at an injustice, my great-aunt's gravelly voice. I no longer have the mementos that old woman gave me. What I do have are her stories of the wind and the Laramie Basin where we lived.

～ ～ ～

I think of her when I read about Aeolus, in Greek mythology, who lived in a cave of winds. Aeolus tied up the winds in a bag for the wandering Ulysses, and Ulysses' men untied the bag and freed the winds. This woman was a modern Aeolus, and I was a thin shadow of Ulysses, outbound on a voyage from child-hood to adulthood.

When we met, she seemed ancient to me. Probably she was in her late sixties or early seventies. My best friend's mother had some business—volun-teer or church work—with her at the stone house, and my friend and I had come along for the ride. We had been told to be good girls, and to be quiet, as Mrs. Sands wasn't partial to children. We were good, and we were quiet, though that didn't stop us from making faces at each other and staring at the old woman when she wasn't looking.

Her deeply tanned and wrinkled face looked like saddle leather, and her rhinestone-studded hairnet made it appear as if raindrops had caught and frozen on her white hair. Her face was bony and her nose was long and pointy. Distinctly blue eyes stared coolly back at us as she caught us looking at her. My friend's mother went to the car for something and that was when the old woman marched out to the kitchen and came back carrying a plate of chocolate chip cookies, which she thumped down on the loveseat where the two of us sat.

"What are your names?" she barked, her hands on her hips. She wore a blue-flowered apron over her pink housedress and nylons. "What do you call yourselves? What do they call you at school?"

We answered meekly.

She guessed our ages, twelve, and proceeded to quiz us about life. We told her what we knew, which was little, having lived only the dozen years. She sat down in the Queen Anne chair beside us and listened as though we were specialists.

Emboldened, my friend asked her about the oblong gray and orange rocks on her cherry dining room table. One was about as long and thick as my arm, and the others were smaller with an odd, vein-like texture. The rough rocks definitely looked out of place resting on the polished table. Why were they there? Were they special?

"They're dinosaur bones from Como Bluff, the graveyard of dinosaurs," came the answer. The smaller pieces were possibly triceratops frill, but she wasn't sure yet and would have to do more research.

I would have liked to hear more, but my friend with her short attention span continued with her questions: What was the name of the big blue-gray cat sprawled on the hall carpet? How much did he weigh?

"Job," came the answer. "As in the Book of. About thirty pounds."

How did they make this house? Why is that knotted string hanging on the wall? Do you have any children? Will the cat bite? Does he like dogs? How old are you?

The old woman shook her head impatiently. "Too many questions," she said. "Here, you, quiet one, you pick one question and I will answer it."

I blushed and looked to my friend for guidance.

The old woman shook her head. "Come on, child. You have a mind of your own, don't you? Of course you do. There isn't any right question. This isn't a quiz, you know."

"Fine," I said, slightly miffed. Just because I was quiet and shy didn't mean I was brain-dead. If she only knew how smart I thought I was. "What is that knotted thing on the wall?"

"This," the old woman said, "is a wind-keeper." She went over to the wall and lifted the string carefully off its hook. It was a length of thick, gray household string about six inches long, tied into three knots of different sizes: one the size of a marble, the next about the size of a large gumball, the last about the size of a golf ball.

"It's a copy I made," she said. "My grandmother brought the original from Finland when she came to farm Dakota Territory. She said it was the custom when she was a girl to hang a wind-keeper in the house to keep the winds from blowing too hard. Do you know what will happen if the knots are untied?"

We shook our heads.

"The first knot keeps the small winds at bay," she said. "If you untie it, you let loose the breezes." Deftly she picked apart the small knot until that end of the string lay open and kinky in her hard, shiny hand.

"Untie the middle knot and you unleash the middling winds." Painstakingly, with some stiffness in her bony knuckles, she unpacked the knobby middle knot. After a few moments the middle of the length of string lay mostly straight in her hand, with just a few crimps.

"And this knot—"she held up the string to show the largest and last of them—"This knot holds the chinook winds, the Santa Anas, the *mistrals,* and the *foehns.*" "Ferns," we heard her say, and I imagined huge smothering fronds floating down like green parachutes on some person named Santa Ana in the mist.

Her fingers picked at the clump of string, rubbing, pulling, coaxing the knot apart. The knot looked hard and tightly woven, impossible to untie. But she did it and held the result out triumphantly. My friend's mother had come in and was watching too. We stared at the crinkled string lying in the old woman's palm. Just a length of common household string. Was she making fools of us? Uncertain, yet polite to the end, my friend and I smiled and nodded.

"It's not the Beaufort scale," the old woman admitted. "I'm afraid it's a little less than scientific."

Nods again.

Quickly she retied the string in ways I hadn't learned in months of tying clove hitches and sailor's knots with my Girl Scout troop. She held the re-knotted string up in the air like an auctioneer. "Who shall keep it?" she called out. "Who shall be the keeper of the winds?"

Silence. We looked at each other. Who did this nutty old woman think she was kidding? Reluctantly I held out my hand. She gave me the length of knotted string and I tucked it in my coat pocket and left it there.

That night a big wind came into the valley. It whined at the windows and doors and threw itself against the house. All night long the wind blew, shaking the floors and fanning the curtains at our tightly-closed windows. I didn't sleep much. In the morning the wind had moved on. In its wake, shingles lay scattered on the lawns and prairie, pried off our roof and our neighbors' roofs as if by a giant knife. Down in what we called the "tree area" of Laramie, branches covered the streets. Near my school, a cottonwood branch as thick as a man's torso had broken off and buried itself in the roof of a car.

I dug the knotted string out of my coat pocket and locked it up in the little red cedar box I'd bought at Mount Rainer National Park. I never untied that string after that. I rarely even took it out of the box. The old woman had made me a believer in her grandmother's wind-keeper from Finland just as the sailors centuries ago had believed their safety on the sea lay in the hands of Finnish wind witches and wind wizards.

That was the beginning of my acquaintance with the old woman. No one living in Laramie now can remember her given name. She used her married name, what she called her "public name," like a shield. Woe to the person under forty who didn't address her as Mrs. Sands. Few knew she had a private name. Fewer still knew what it was.

When I grew to know her a little better, she told me she'd renamed herself after her husband died of Parkinson's disease. She'd taken care of him for five years and after his death she was just about dead herself. She ran off to Sheep Mountain west of Laramie. Members of her church as well as her neighbors all thought she'd gone to Florida to nurse an old friend. That was what women like her did, after all—took care of others and never themselves. Never mind trying to recover one's own life and learning how to live and make choices again. It just wasn't done.

So it was strange enough that she'd climbed the mountain. Stranger still, while camping up there, she planned the rest of her life. Until that time she'd always been the kind of person who did what was expected of her. But from then on, she was going to do what she wanted. To celebrate this new person she was going to become, she looked in the book she'd brought and found a new name for herself: Nasim, a gentle breeze that travels the sands of the Middle East. She spoke it aloud to the sky: "Nah-SEEM." Yes, that would do.

I guess she saw in me a pupil. She decided she would teach me: about the winds, about the land we lived on, about the flowers and the wildlife that needed the land around us. Maybe she sensed, beneath my cold shyness, a love for the land that matched her own, and a similar desire for knowledge and for mystery, both. Or maybe she saw my great ignorance as a challenge.

∾ ∾ ∾

Someday my great-grandchildren and I will sit down together and I will begin a story like this: "Listen, dear ones. When I was a child in Wyoming…." Then I will unknot a string of words and the children won't be sure whether I am kidding or serious, telling the truth or creating fiction.

Whether they believe me or not will perhaps depend on what shape the world is in. Will tales of open prairies and wildlands have become myth? Will the story of a child allowed to run free out on the land, alone with her dog, seem implausible? What will the children of my future know and experience? When I tell them about the west as I knew it, will they believe me?

Will I want them to believe me, if it means they will see the extent of their generation's loss by comparing my stories to their reality?

During another visit to the stone house, Nasim allowed my friend and me to examine other dinosaur fossils she had found over the years. She pointed out one rectangular fossil which she said had originally been a slab of soft river mud. A dinosaur of some kind had rested on the mud and left a print of its scaly skin. The mud had hardened and other rocks had covered it, protecting the print until the day Nasim unearthed it on a hike near the town of Medicine Bow, Wyoming. We touched the imprint gingerly; so delicate, it looked as though even the winds of our breaths would blow it away.

The next treasure she handed over, a nondescript light brown stone, looked like a common rock found in a parking lot. When she pointed out the tiny etched ridges in the stone and told us they were the fossilized remains of blood vessels, I wondered if I had passed by similar rocks on my wanderings on the prairie, not knowing their true origin. Maybe I had overlooked entire skeletons of dinosaurs and never known it.

We must have looked unimpressed, however, because Nasim put down the fossils and took off the reading glasses she'd been wearing. "Can you even fathom that the dinosaurs lived on this planet for millions of years?" she asked us. "Think of it—we humans have been here only for the blink of a geologic eye, the raindrop of a geologic ocean."

We looked at her dumbly. What did she expect of us? To be able to fathom the span of time of the earth's existence? We had been born shortly after John F. Kennedy's inauguration. Nixon was president now and Watergate was a mystery to us, one being unearthed in the newspapers. The Vietnam War, a war for us in name only, was practically over. Ours was the world of the Partridge Family, the Brady Bunch, Little Kiddles, and Easy Bake Ovens.

She sighed, pushed aside the fossils, and said it was time for tea. A fly rocketed around the kitchen, buzzing loudly and ricocheting off the shiny white cabinets, as we sat down at the kitchen table. She set out three china cups and filled them with steaming Constant Comment tea. As I scooped spoonfuls of sugar into my cup and stirred the golden red liquid, I thought about what she'd said. That our lives as humans were small and short, and that the time span of the entire existence of humans on earth was brief, seemed as unfathomable to me as the idea of dinosaurs stomping across the Laramie Basin for millions of years. The fly swooped and circled in random loops, bringing me back to the present.

"It was a different world in the days of the dinosaurs," Nasim said. She spooned more sugar into her delicate thistle-flowered teacup. "Wetter, rainier. No flowers, no fruit."

"My dad says the summers are getting hotter and the winters are less snowy," said my friend.

"Oh, dear, that fly wants to land in my tea," Nasim said.

"Want me to kill it, Mrs. Sands?" my friend asked.

"No, no," Nasim said. "I'll let it out the door." She opened the kitchen door, made little swooshing motions with her hands, and the fly flew outside.

"Think of a fly," she said, settling back down at the table. "And you can picture the length of human existence on this planet. The fly, let's say, is born, lives, and dies in the span of seven days. If those seven days happen to be sunny and windy, for all the fly knows it has always been sunny and windy and always will be. It doesn't know that the day before it was hatched, rain fell, and the day after it died, rain fell."

"My dad is not a fly," my friend sputtered.

I giggled and sipped my tea.

"I know, honey," Nasim said. "You're missing the point. Have another cookie."

Listen now, dear ones: while we are in sunshine, I will untie a knot in the wind keeper and begin the story as the winds blow.

～ ～ ～

Wyoming is a huge old crazy quilt. Rivers stitch the umber and gold grasslands to the gray rock mountains. Olive green sagebrush scrublands edge the dark green embroidery of ponderosa pine forests. Patches of cool blue water join to larger patches of bare red dirt, seamed by the Continental Divide. Colors of deep sky blue, olive gray green, brick red, gray blue, deep gold, hunter, silver appear in great blocks or in strips side by side. The piece I knew and loved as a child was a small part of the quilt, a plain part, a part sometimes overlooked compared to the rest of Wyoming.

In the part of Wyoming that I love best, the Medicine Bow Mountains mark the western boundary, beyond which the sun walks without me. To the north, Laramie Peak can be seen on clear days, rising like a shimmering blue pyramid. To the south, layers of blue foothills and white peaks above them form a wall of beauty, and to the east, the worn-down hump of the Laramie Range squats like an old goddess of Malta. Names such as Rawah, Sierra Madre, and Neversummer surround my patch on maps.

Here in the middle, in the basin between the mountains, the people gather, the trains mournfully call, the cattle and antelope graze—a silent majority —while shadows of clouds run across the land. Here the winds meet, let loose by Ulysses' foolish sailors.

Homer celebrated the four wind gods of Greek mythology: Boreas, the north wind, strong and sharply cold; Notos, the south wind that carries warm rains; Euros, the old east wind; and Zephyros, the gentle west wind. It seems every culture has named the winds, whether they are counted as four, five, eight, or more. The hot, dry winds are known as the *simoom* in the Middle East, as the *haboob* in the Sudan, as the *zonda* in Argentina, and as the *khamsin* in Egypt. The gentle breezes, siblings of Zephyros, are known as *kohilo* in Hawaii, *waff* in Scotland, *nasim* in Arabia, and *feh* in Shanghai.

There are names for dry northerly winds and names for wet northeasterly winds and names for just plain easterly or westerly winds. They roll off the tongue like music: *hawa shimali, gallego, tramontana, narai; bora, koshava, crivetz, buran; steppenwind, tegenwind, mistral,* and *monsoon.*

When I was young in Wyoming, I named the winds too, and I gave them personalities—usually malicious or mischievous ones, rarely gentle. The first wind I named came in summer, the shortest season in Wyoming. I called it the grass comb wind, for the way it ran through the grassy hair of the Laramie Basin.

I came to Wyoming with the grass comb wind. I had spent my early childhood in the womb of the midwest, surrounded by trees and humidity and rich black river bottom soil that could grow any seed, no matter how hard its shell. My life there was as calm and slow as a hazy summer morning. The prospect of moving to Wyoming broke the glassy stillness in which I lived.

Suddenly, or so it seemed to me, my father, a professor of economics, announced he'd gotten a new job as a dean at the University of Wyoming. A month later, we were moving to Laramie. We had traveled through Wyoming once when I was in kindergarten, but I remembered nothing of it. Wyoming sounded exotic and wild. I imagined Laramie as a dusty wooden town beneath a great red cliff with a huge blue sky stretched above it. The townspeople rode horses, cattle ran through the streets, and everyone wore cowboy hats.

I was right about the sky. It was huge and blue.

We drove west for two days and cheered when we crossed the Wyoming state line. Miles later we reached Cheyenne and stopped for gas. It was July but the wind felt autumn-cold, and we put on our jackets. Cheyenne was disappointing. It slumped, comatose; the hilly bumps rising on its western edge were poor excuses for mountains to peak-eager flatlanders.

Outside Cheyenne the land sloped gradually upwards, a great ramp of ancient sediments. This rising ground is all that remains of the ancestral Rocky Mountains, high peaks that gradually eroded long before humans came onto the scene. From the rubble rose the "new" Rocky Mountains we see today. Even as we crossed the granite backbone of the Laramie Range, part of the Rocky Mountains and over a billion years old, these rocks, too, were slowly eroding, and would become rubble again in another million years or so.

At the summit, a giant bronze head of Abraham Lincoln smiled sadly down upon the interstate. Created by sculptor Robert Russin, it marked the highest point of elevation, 8,835 feet, on the old Lincoln Highway, the first transcontinental highway. When I-80 replaced the Lincoln Highway in 1969, the bust was moved about a mile to stand over the rest area next to the interstate.

Winding down Telephone Canyon, the highway cut through steep rock walls, exposing dark red sandstone cliffs. We noticed a drastic difference in vegetation on the right and left sides of the steep canyon slopes. On the moister, north-facing side to our left, tall ponderosa pines and Douglas firs covered the land. On the drier, south-facing side of the canyon, shrubs and stunted pines grew. Lower down, they were replaced by grasses, sagebrush, and an occasional yucca. We didn't know it at that moment, but the south-facing side with its dry, scrubby vegetation was more typical of our future home than the other side with its lush pines and firs.

Truck drivers checked their brakes, then barreled past us. We flew past a boy riding a skateboard on the shoulder of the highway. A yellow Cadillac with tail fins cruised beside him. The boy was frozen to the skateboard, going faster than any skateboard was ever meant to go, but he didn't fall as he swooped around a curve of the highway. Leaving him behind, we cut through gray marine limestone and, farther on, more red sandstone as we came out of the mountains and into the foothills. These hills had once been sand dunes beside an ancient sea, long before the dinosaurs even existed. Suddenly the highway left the canyon's protective folds and spilled out onto the vast green expanse of the Laramie Basin.

Miles of shortgrass bent to the wind's teeth as it ruffled the heads of the warm-season grasses by the road, then whipped alkaline grit up onto the windshield. In the distance rose a blue mass of mountains, and to the south white peaks sparkled. The land shimmered in green. Where was my red cliff? My dusty wood buildings beneath it?

A dark blot seeped across the green upslope of the basin and, as we drove nearer, resolved into buildings and trees. Dwarfed by the vast basin in which it lay, Laramie looked low to the ground, beaten down, scuffed. We crossed the city limits and soon found that our new yard was treeless, as was our street, as was our entire side of town. Patches of bare ground appeared, some areas white with gypsum, some areas rusty orange with pulverized sandstone. When we got out of our car, the wind was blowing so hard we could barely stand up.

A hundred years earlier, another traveler looking at the Laramie Basin for the first time felt the same disappointment I felt that day and recorded it for the *New York Times* in June 1869, according to Wyoming historian T. A. Larsen. "[W]hat a scene of desolation met our view and surrounded us... a vast barren basin utterly destitute of life...."

But we were both wrong. Even the most barren of rocks, the hottest of deserts, the coldest of polar seas support some life. Rachel Carson wrote of scientists returning to the island of Krakatoa years after a violent eruption there had paved the land in lava. They found plants and insects at work repopulating the island, creating life on the bare rock surface. Most had been wind-borne.

In Wyoming, I was wind born, brought to life by the wind and the open land. Unlike that earlier traveler, I found life in that "barren basin." Inner life and outer life became stitched together, so that what I was didn't seem to end at the skin, but was part grass, part rock, part sego lily, part sagebrush, part meadowlark, part sky.

And then I grew up and forgot.

S_{ILK} W_{IND}

*End of summer,
beginning of autumn*

By chance our family built a house at the edge of town. Beyond us was nothing much of human origin except a log house to the southeast where a square-dancing club met. About a mile to the northeast one could spot a rancher's house and outbuildings, where Mr. Lamb and his wife lived, and at about half that distance lay a skeet shooting range, used in July and August. The rest was open prairie.

My brother and I soon realized our great fortune: it was not our parents' way to live at the edge of a town, but somehow we'd ended up there. And we savored our luck to the fullest.

Our legal backyard was a narrow margin of cultivated land, a strip of bluegrass sod and flowers that my mother planted. Red California poppies, white

Shasta daisies, delicate purple harebells, coral lady's hearts, pungent mint—she nursed them through the wicked snowy spring. Finally stems burst out of the red-brown soil in May and by late June and early July blossoms tumbled across the rough dirt, blooming in spite of the dry winds and the strong sunlight.

Our borrowed backyard was a wide margin of wild, uncultivated land, a swath of wild buffalo grass. The Prairie, we called it. "We're going out on the Prairie," my brother Mark and I would yell to our mother as we ran out the back door. To those whose job it is to know better, that Prairie is also known as shortgrass prairie, shortgrass plain, sagebrush steppe, sagebrush shrubland, or any combination of terms, depending on variations in soil quality, vegetation, and rainfall.

But the Prairie it was to us. It opened behind our house, dipped and curved past the skeet shooting range and log house, rose slightly by the rancher's house, then rose more steeply into the Laramie Mountains. It was our backyard, laboratory, and playground, and my brother and I, accompanied by my Australian shepherd dog, explored every rising foot of it. It shaped our bodies as we ran; it shaped our minds, our thoughts, and our imaginations as we played. We took rocks from it and gave them back. We took flowers and grasshoppers from it and didn't give them back. From the stone circle set into the hillside, my own little haven, to the old junk pits, my brother's haven, to the hogbacks rising toward the mountains, to the red hills northward, to the scrub pine gullies further east, the land schooled us better than the Laramie public schools did. It was the best place to be as a child. That rough, left-alone land appealed to the spirit in ways that no carefully planned and planted park ever could.

Once it had been ranch land, either Lamb's or someone else's, where skinny cattle wintered and grew fatter in the summer. Perhaps it was on this very stretch of range that the legend of the Plains cattle industry's origins began. Local history relates that one Tom Alsop, foreman of a bull team en route from Omaha to Salt Lake, ran into a snowstorm on Sherman Hill east of Laramie in December of 1863. He cut loose the oxen team and set them free—to die, he thought—and rode back to Omaha. But in the spring they were found, still alive, grazing on the grasses of the Laramie Basin. No one up north had tried leaving cattle to fend for themselves during the winter, for fear they would die. But now, by surviving, these oxen had inadvertently jump-started the range cattle industry on the northern Plains.

Today some botanists might point to evidence of abuse of the land in the prevalence of sagebrush and prickly pear. Overgrazing leaves such clues. And the land had been dumped on, too: witness my brother's favorite place on the prairie—the two long, mysterious pits full of pieces of old furniture and machinery, rusted metal, and fractured crockery. Mark and I scavenged those pits, salvaging whatever we could bring home without an uproar from our parents—pieces of scrap metal, twisted and lace-thin from rust; shards of lavender and amethyst-colored glass; old brown and green glass insulators; a wooden chair; an old china plate.

My favorite place, however, was pristine, untouched by human hands—a stone circle about a mile or more from our house, across open prairie. Set partially into a hill, this natural rock-walled enclosure was my destination on childhood walks, and I knew each ledge and rock. I was never sure how the circle had formed, whether it had been an old overgrown quarry or perhaps an ancient pool or even a small meteor crater. All I knew was that it was a magical place, my open-air palace, stunning in spring and summer when the floor of the circle was covered with patches of purple and yellow wildflowers. When we perched there on the ledges, my dog and I could see for miles.

Though others before us may have appreciated this rising prairie at the east edge of the Laramie Basin for financial reasons, Mark and I loved the prairie on its own terms, with the passion that only two young introverts could bring to it. Doomed as social misfits by our shyness, our love of books, and our weird non-Anglo-Saxon family name, we found redemption in the land's secret beauties and acceptance in its wide-open spaces. In school we were clumsy; on the prairie we moved lightly and quietly, two young sun-browned animals.

In the summer, though cattle no longer grazed this range, sheep still wandered with the sheepherder and his silver-colored sheepwagon. They clustered like a dun-colored cloud on the red hills north of us. As the sheep grazed, the whole side of the hill seemed to ripple like a living, breathing animal. After a few days, they'd move on. When the hill was bare once again, I'd take my dog over and follow her as she trotted excitedly back and forth in the dust. Perhaps the lingering smell of the flock triggered in her the desire, planted in her genes, to nip heels, to start a chain reaction of sheep, to command for once, instead of being commanded. She would herd a few ghost sheep, look at the horizon wistfully where they had gone, and then we'd run on. On to our favorite places, the circuit we traced like a faint songline from the dreaming time: red hills, sandstone blocks, old rock wall circle, junk pits, then across rough ground for home.

This dog was a native of Wyoming, born in the old Laramie dog pound, a damp concrete building slumped into the moist ground where the Laramie River curves north of town. I volunteered to work there the year I was eleven, and promptly fell in love with a litter of Australian shepherd puppies, slated to be put to sleep in a few weeks. I had to have them all. My parents allowed me one, a tailless black puppy with brown tiger-striped paws.

I took her home and started walking her every day on the sidewalk down our street. Neighbors laughed to see me with the clumsy black fluff of a pup, no larger than a guinea pig. When she reached the size of a small cat I began to take her out on the prairie. Soon she grew tall enough to see over the smaller sagebrush and agile enough to jump over the larger ones.

As I walk now on the prairie, I think of her and how I abandoned her when I left home. Dumped on my parents, she ended up moving with them to the green farming country of the Genesee Valley south of Lake Ontario, where she chased New York squirrels across a lush green lawn until her death at age seventeen. She is buried beneath an apple orchard, she who had seen only three trees in all her time in Wyoming. I wondered if it was strange for her, moving to a place where trees grew and one lawn merged into another lawn into another; I wondered if she missed the wildness of the prairie, running without fences or roads in her way, feeling the wind stroke her silky black fur. I'll never know.

In ancient China and India, the dog was associated with movement, and with the realm above the soil where clouds sail and rain gathers. My dog will always be connected, for me, with the prairie, the wind, the smell of sagebrush, the red soil, though she lies beneath lush grass and apple blossoms in western New York State.

As I walk now on the prairie, alone without her, I think of that move to New York State, where Eric, the youngest of my three siblings, spent his formative years. To him, southern Wyoming is a dry, dusty badlands compared with the meadows and vineyards and glacial lakes of his childhood in the Genesee Valley. Now and then I am surprised by the differences between us, the three older ones raised in Wyoming, and him, the youngest, raised in the east. Maybe the differences occur simply because of the genetic throw of the dice that makes him who he is. Maybe it's because he's eight years younger than I. Then again, perhaps it's because of the different landscapes we encountered during our early years, printing their individual stamps on us. His was a landscape of bounty, where grapevines grew on hillsides above the Finger Lakes, where orchards in the fall produced dozens of varieties of apples, in every shade of red and gold, where orange daylilies that had to be nurtured in Wyoming grew as weeds along the roads.

My brother Mark, my sister Marilyn, and I, however, remember biting winds, gardens planted that never grew, and searing sunlight that turned the whole Laramie Valley brown in August, bleaching it to a pale gold by September.

I remember one silk-wind afternoon of autumn, many years past, when the three of us got off the school bus. We were free for the rest of the golden day. My sister headed off with her friends. Mark and I started home, intending to dump our backpacks and then head out onto the prairie.

Suddenly our way was blocked. The kids who had been harassing us daily on the school bus, whom we had tried to ignore, had gotten tired of our passivity. Their taunts at me turned to pushes at my brother. He dropped his backpack and was soon rolling on the ground with a boy older and bigger than him. How I wanted to wade in and smack that boy, smack the whole lot of them. But I just stood there and let their insults cut and bruise me, a coward at twelve, while my brother fought a battle he wasn't going to win.

Then I heard a car door slam. A streak of white hair, blue housedress, and black oxfords flew to the scene. Nasim grabbed the boy on top of Mark and lifted him off by his shirt collar, although he was about as big as she was. "Stop it at once!" she shouted at the crowd of kids watching. "You should be ashamed of yourselves, you narrow, bovine-minded dung worms. Get on home, all of you, or I'll call your parents and send the police to your homes." The crowd scattered. Nasim helped my brother up and dusted off his shirt. With her handkerchief she wiped the blood and mucous off his face, then walked with him to her car. "Is that all you can do, just stand there?" she yelled at me. "Pick up his things and get in."

Nasim dropped us off at our house. She was on her Meals-on-Wheels delivery route to the homebound oldsters and had to hurry on before the meals in the hot box in her back seat got cold. It was Chinese food that day—I could smell the sweet and sour pork and fried rice. She gave us each a fortune cookie.

"Food for thought," she said grimly.

Inside, while our mother fussed and cleaned Mark's scrapes, I cried in my room. Life was so unfair. Why had Nasim yelled at me? I had been just an innocent bystander. Later, I came down and sat with my brother at the kitchen table to open our fortune cookies. His read, "You will win a million dollars." Mine read, "You must do the thing you are afraid to do." I suggested to him that maybe our fortune cookies had gotten mixed up, and his was really mine. Mark looked at mine and said he didn't think so. Then our mother looked at mine and said she had always told me that, and maybe I could try to start sticking up for myself now. I stared out the window and felt very sorry for myself.

When I think of that incident now, I remember working in a library with two red-haired women, one the librarian, the other a clerk. Their red hair was the only thing they had in common besides the hate they felt for each other. Every morning, the clerk turned on her computer and retrieved the same document: a letter of resignation. Every morning she typed in that day's date at the top, replacing the previous date, and printed out the letter, ready to hand to the librarian just before the librarian fired her—although the librarian never did. The letters stacked up, five per week, in her desk drawer.

Had Nasim, in some strange way, foreseen my need for that fortune and saved that cookie for me, ready to present at the right moment? Who knows? I didn't believe in coincidence at the time. I savored the magic of that fortune's appearance and thought about its message until I finally lost the slip of paper, as I lost so many things I held dear. Careless girl.

Wherever one's childhood home, it provides a place from which to launch oneself into the world. Then it becomes a place to return to, a place to measure change, to clock the passage of time. That is, for some people. Although Mark loved the prairie we roamed, he has not returned to Laramie since he left over twenty years ago. He has said he will never go back there again. The Tetons and Yellowstone are his "prairie" now; Laramie is just an exit where he refuels his truck on the way.

On the other hand, I left Laramie and have returned so many times that I feel like some kind of migratory bird with a magnetized skull, drawn back to this place season after season. The writer Bruce Chatwin, the original modern nomad, said that that state of movement is the most natural one in humans—our urge to wander, and our urge to return to the sites of previous wanderings.

And so in autumn I come back again to Laramie. On this day I sit by Spring Creek to watch cottonwood leaves twist on their flat stems in the breeze. One leaf flutters, then another, another, and soon the whole tree is shimmering like a golden fountain of fire.

Cottonwoods are the water witches of the west. "Water nearby," their pale branches whisper. The Plains tribes found the sweet inner bark useful as food, and tea from the bark was supposed to cure colds. The cottonwood's leaves with their healing chemicals were applied to the skin as a poultice for sores and bruises. It is the season when leaves float down like small golden boats riding the waves of a great blue lake. No two leaves touch ground at exactly the same time. The light has a rich quality that painters dream of, and people come out of their homes and offices to touch and be touched by this light.

It is rare to find air so still here. I hold my breath—will the wind start up again? Easy, easy. For once we may rest. In autumn, storms dwindle, lose the power of the summer's Gulf moisture that earlier had pushed the clouds and rain this far north.

But the next afternoon as I stand with my sister-in-law, Kristen, and my ten-year-old son, Adam, on a rocky lakeshore on the back of the Laramie Range, the wind comes up. Thunder cracks across the piled mounds of pink granite above us, and the wind scatters rain like clear seeds around us. We help Adam tie a lure to his fishing line. To the west, the sun bores a hole in the dark purple clouds, turning the falling rain around us into sheets of aluminum. Lightning ripples across the sky and thunder shakes the granite bones of the mountain range beneath our feet.

Quickly he casts his line, an arc of silver, across the circle of dark blue: everyday geometry up here in the mountains, I think. We wait, crouching by the lake, soaked. He reels in, casts again. No good.

More lightning falls, like a white ribbed curtain all around us. Thunder jolts our bones. Here we are, risking our lives, for what? A fish. Three big pale fish, that's us. We should leave before a burning hook of lightning snags all of us and pulls us gasping and writhing out of this world.

But we wait, stupidly, full of the kind of hope that gamblers feel. We women watch as he casts again. The lure sails far out onto the rain-peppered lake. Were I truly a fish, I'd have taken cover near the bottom of the lake. But no. Something is aware and curious and grabs the line. We yell. Adam expertly reels it in, well taught by his father and his uncles.

It's a short path to death: a straight line to shore and a boy who wants more than anything at this moment to catch this fish. He pulls it out of the water. At the end of the tenuous line hangs a sleek package of silver. It struggles for breath; its tail lifts as if to push away the painful hook. To our thunder-jolted, lightning-bleached brains, it seems that the silver water has fused with the sunlight, and, given spirit by the wind's rainy breath, become a living thing. The catalyst of hook and line completes its creation and its death as well.

The fish gasps, then, feeling earth beneath it, flops against the rocks on the shore. A small rainbow trout, until now it was as unaware of being submerged in water as we are unaware of being submerged in air. Fish do not "see" water except when it moves the sands and gravel beneath them, or when a strong current pushes against their fins. We do not "see" air, except when it moves through trees, scatters dust, brushes grass and hair. Only when the air currents flow, like rivers and streams around us, are we aware of the medium in which we live. We live in an ocean, an ocean of air.

In this ocean, the air is densest at the bottom, the surface of the planet, where land meets sea. As one climbs in elevation, the air becomes thinner. When I was a child in the high, thin air of Laramie, one of the many nomadic college football coaches using the University of Wyoming as a stepping stone to a warmer climate ordered a sign painted in the stands of the foot-ball stadium opposite the visiting team's bench. It said something like, "Welcome to 7,250 feet above sea level." More than an actual measurement, the sign said in essence, "Welcome to football in the stratosphere, suckers. Did you remember your oxygen tanks?"

Adam thumps the back of the fish's head against a rock. The fish lies still. Utterly soaked, we grab fish and pole and bucket and run across the wet rocks to the shelter of the car.

Large enough to keep but too small to brag about, the fish nevertheless deserves our attention, I say, thinking out loud as we drive home. That it was swimming near the lake's surface rather than taking cover deeper, that we were out in the rain and light-ning rather than taking cover in the car—I tell my son that the story could have come out differently.

My son shrugs. He believes there's a God who throws dice to determine the outcome of events. It's what my son would do if he were in charge of the universe. Impersonal, arbitrary, scrupulously impar-tial is his God. The roll of the dice was simply in our favor today.

Back in the Laramie kitchen of my husband's parents, we tell the others of our adventure, of stand-ing in the middle of a thunderstorm risking all for a little fish. They laugh. My son cleans the fish, we cook it in a frying pan, and carefully debone it before dividing it up. There is just enough for a little bit for my sister-in-law, a little bit for me, and a larger bit for my son. My small piece of fish feels like a communion wafer on my tongue. I close my eyes and swallow.

RATTLESNAKE WIND

Full autumn

THE WIND IS blowing, trying to round off the corners of the house. Sprinkling dust against the windows, it swishes in the dry grasses like a rattlesnake seeking somewhere warm to curl. It shakes the rabbitbrush blossoms, scattering yellow flowers among the sagebrush like feathers scattered after a kill. In town it whisks the gold dust of the fallen locust leaves into piles in the gutters and rattles the twisted seed pods. Carrier of dust and seeds, this wind holds death and life in its teeth.

One blue evening when I was thirteen, I was waiting on a Laramie street for my mother to pick me up, when the wind rose and began to clatter in the cottonwood trees surrounding the county courthouse nearby—an eerie, cold sound. The streets were empty of traffic. Everyone had gone home except for the prisoners on the top floor of the courthouse. I waited, feeling abandoned. My mother was late. I wanted so much to be home, to walk out past the house into the great space where no trees or buildings could throw shadows, where nothing could block my line of sight, where no one could hide. But I was stuck, it was getting cold, and I suspected that maybe this time she'd forgotten me.

I looked up at the top floor of the courthouse to the south, at the bars on the windows, and saw a face. For a minute I wasn't sure which person was behind bars, the one up there with a view of the town and surrounding valley, or me down below, trapped among the houses and trees. I wanted to run away. Then I saw her walking down the front steps of the courthouse, buttoning her sensible navy blue car coat. Nasim.

"Hey!" I yelled. "Hello!"

She looked over, saw me, and started walking in my direction across the courthouse lawn.

"What were you doing in there?" I asked.

"Seeing a friend," she said.

"In jail?" I gasped.

"Yes, dear, in jail."

"What did he do wrong?"

"She," Nasim said, noting my reaction. "And nothing you need to concern yourself with. What are you doing here? It's getting dark."

"I'm waiting for my mother to pick me up. I was at the orthodontist."

"Do you need a ride?" she asked.

"No, because then she'll show up and she won't find me here."

"Then I'll wait with you until she comes, hon." She sat down on the curb, tucked her dress discreetly over her legs, wrapped her coat around her, then plopped her big black pocketbook across her knees.

I sat down beside her. "What's it like up there?" I pointed to the prison windows.

"Dark. Small. Smelly. Like a cave."

"Will your friend be there long?" I asked, trying to worm more information out of her.

"I don't know. If she would just call a lawyer, she'd be out tonight or tomorrow. But she won't call one."

"Why not?" I asked.

"Because then she would be out tonight or tomorrow. And they'd put her back where she usually is, in the nursing home," she said, again noting my surprise.

"What did she do wrong?"

Nasim sighed and I wondered if I'd been too nosy. Then she straightened her coat, pulled a clean white handkerchief out of her pocket, and dabbed her nose. "She got into a delivery van at the nursing home, drove it to a jewelry store, and tried to hold up the store. She had a curling iron in her pocket, which she told them was a gun. They laughed at her, so she smashed their display case with her purse. She had just snagged a diamond bracelet with her curling iron when the police arrived."

"Wow. A jewel thief. How old is she?" I asked.

"Eighty-six. And she is not a jewel thief. She used to teach high school mathematics back east. She's always been active until just a few years ago, when all her health problems seemed to hit her at once. Before that, she traveled, studied art history and archaeology, and even got arrested protesting at nuclear power plants in the sixties. Now she's stuck in little ol' Laramie in a nursing home, no friends living anymore, except me, no family either, and now the big event of the day is dinner, when you find out who died that day."

We sat there quietly for a few minutes, then I said, "Well, at least she's going out fighting."

Nasim laughed, but it wasn't a happy laugh. "Hit me over the head, push me off a cliff at Vedauwoo, abandon me out on the prairie up at Shirley Basin, but don't, for God's sake, ever let me end up stuck in a nursing home."

"You won't," I said, in my most reassuring voice.

She laughed again and patted my hand. "Barely a decade or so of living under your belt and yet you think you can reassure me? Able to foretell the future, eh?"

I ignored her. "Why a jewelry store?"

"I don't know. Me, I would have just taken that van and kept on driving until it ran out of gas."

I looked up at the windows, now faintly lit from within. "Can she see us?"

"No. Those windows face a large hallway, not the cells. The cells are on the other side of the building."

"I saw somebody's face," I said.

"Maybe it was mine," she said. "I did stop at the window to see what the view was like toward the Ivinson mansion."

"Was it any good?"

"Beautiful," she said. "Just beautiful. I felt like a bird flying above the town."

We sat together on the curb, waiting. The wind slowed. Two large black crows landed in the cotton-woods and perched on the top branches, as though waiting with us.

"It's getting dark," I said, shivering. "I hate the dark."

"I don't mind the dark. When I close my eyes in the dark, sometimes I see a great open space," Nasim said, scrunching up her shoulders. Suddenly she seemed much smaller than me. And more fragile. "It's feature-less and fuzzy, but somehow I can feel that it has depth and that it's hard. It stretches for miles between my corneas and my eyelids. I keep trying to see what's there."

We sat some more, still waiting. The wind stopped entirely. The crows didn't move.

"I like being in the dark in an auditorium," she said, "Just before the curtains rise. Or when I'm in a concert hall waiting for the orchestra to play, between movements, but there's that glorious silence for a moment. The violins and cellos almost stop vibrating and the metal of the trumpets and flutes cools just a lit-tle, then the conductor takes a breath—"

"I've heard that too," I said.

"It's an empty space, but it demands as much of the audience as the music does," Nasim said.

"Like the empty space you see when you close your eyes?" I asked.

She smiled. "You keep me young, kiddo."

Silence for a moment. Then I added, "Or the moment between gusts of wind, when the next wave hasn't arrived yet."

"Shhh, it's here," she said, her eyes closed. But just then, as if on cue, the wind came back. With it came my mother in her car. She hadn't forgotten me after all. She returned Nasim's wave, then Nasim headed back across the courthouse lawn. I ran across the parking lot to the warmth of my mother's car, and realized as we drove off that although I had a whole life still to live, Nasim had only a small portion left. But I knew she would squeeze more from those few years than I would manage to get from double that number, because she had imagination and the will to try anything at least once. Me, I was timid, afraid of just about everything. I would make, I decided, a terrible old lady. Not a cool one like Nasim or her friend.

When I remember that the winds are the planet's circulatory and respiratory system, cleansing valleys of air pollution, carrying off tons of dust every year, pollinating myriad plants, carving and eroding entire mountain ranges, my annoyance at being pushed and dusted by gusts diminishes. But then I step out onto open land, ready to walk and look. The wind whips my clothes and rumbles in my ears, and waters my eyes, and instead of merging with the landscape, I feel just how separate I am from it, uprooted like a dried Russian thistle, the rolling tumbleweed. So I get low, crouch among the sagebrush and bunchgrass, and let the Earth's curve shelter me. I listen to the wind flow above me and I feel calm again.

Once I stood on a bridge above the place where two rivers converged. The dark brown waters of one flowed alongside the hazel green waters of the other, like oil touching vinegar. As the turbulence of their two currents churned their waters, each river mixed with the other and the waters continued on as one.

Two winds converge invisibly here in the Laramie Basin. Two rivers of wind, one blowing around the north end of the Medicine Bow Mountains, the other around the south end, meet on the plains near Laramie. You can see it in the lines of settlement. Both south and north of the main part of town, houses are sparse. Trees don't grow, no matter how carefully nurtured, and the few structures there are, both wood frame houses and metal mobile homes, look scarred and battered by the winds.

My brother-in-law, at the time a young entrepreneur in Laramie, was considering whether to buy a building downtown, an old two-story brick one down by the railroad tracks. A structural engineer inspected the building and advised him not to buy, so he didn't. Not one month later, after one of the daily northbound trains roared through town, one side of the building collapsed. The rest of the structure had to be demolished. In the newspaper story about the damage, people blamed the freight trains for not slowing down as they passed through town, and some voiced concerns about the impact of the daily rumble of coal trains on the other old buildings nearby.

I wondered if the wind could have damaged the building. Does its constant battering weaken structures? Or is it only people who are worn down by it? How is the mind's climate affected by the wind? Armenian mythology gave the wind, Ays, a demonic personality. Ays would blow into a human's body and possess it, driving the human to madness. Truly, whether the wind is a demon or just a current of air, it can excite and it can dull. It can irritate and anger. Its presence drives up the profits of saloons and bars. It is one force that humans can't dam, strip, program, plow, dynamite, or break.

Not that people haven't tried. Nasim told me of a tribe in the Middle East whose wells dried up. Hysterical with fear and anger, they searched for something or someone to blame and decided it was the fault of the wind, the hot dry simoom. They declared war on the simoom, marched into the Sahara to battle the wind, and lost. They were never seen again.

Another tribe in the Pacific islands, she said, designated a huge stone the "wind stone," and built a fence around it to keep the winds reined in instead of free to blow. And in India, holy men would walk into windstorms armed with knives, chanting to calm the gales.

Once when we were walking near the Big Hollow, a deep scoop of land between Laramie and Centennial to the west, she showed me how a Cherokee wind wizard could stop a gale. Nasim stopped walking, faced the direction the wind was blowing from, which was west, and put out her hand as if to stop it. Singing softly under her breath, she then turned to the north and pointed in that direction. The wind did not obey. She said a few cuss words. The wind stopped. Momentarily.

She said the Japanese wind god Fujin, who had let the winds out of his big bag when the world was born, and the Hindu wind god Indra could also be coaxed to stop the wind, but she never said how. I did hear her sing a song to the wind another time. It was low and soft, and reminded me of the wind rattling the cottonwood leaves in the trees by the courthouse. She said it wasn't to stop or bind or redirect the wind, but to celebrate it. To celebrate the force that cleanses the air, that pollinates the plants, that breathes for the Earth. To celebrate the wind, because there is nothing one can do to stop it.

Moth Tongue Wind

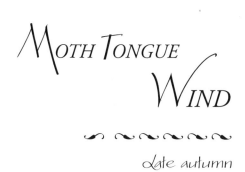

Late autumn

ONE DAY IN October, my middle son Ben and I stretch out on the bank beside Spring Creek and watch the clouds sail by. Like huge flat-bottomed ships they glide overhead, riding the currents. Clouds are the invisible made visible. Invisible vapors surrounding Earth cool and collect in droplet or flake form. They create clouds whose shapes are the signature of their altitude, moisture content, and other characteristics of the air, stable or unstable, in which they were formed. A two-hundred-year-old system for classifying these shapes is still followed today by cloud watchers. It uses three Latin words to name three main types of clouds: cirrus, cumulus, and stratus.

Cirrus clouds are high, thin, and wispy, resembling fibers of cotton. These clouds usually form parallel to each other so that the sky looks like a loom of white yarn waiting to be woven. Cumulus clouds are the fluffy white mounds one sees in the summer sky. In the hot air of afternoon, they rise and double in size like white yeast bread, often becoming high cumulonimbus thunderheads. Stratus clouds form a heavy blanket that the wind cannot tear apart. They are layered—stratified—and are more stable than cirrus or cumulus clouds. Another type, added later to the classification system, is the nimbus cloud, whose Latin root refers to rain or snow. Nimbus clouds are the gray, smudgy ones that so obviously announce the presence of moisture.

These four types intermingle in the sky and in the language to form new varieties of clouds: say them quickly and they sound like a jump rope song, or a chant children might use to choose "It" for a game of tag: "Cirrostratus, cumulostratus; cirrocumulus, cumulonimbus; altocumulus, stratocumulus—you're *It*."

But Ben and I watch the clouds sail past and assign less technical names: dog-with-leg-lifted, lopsided-lion, my-science-teacher's-ear. Slightly dizzy from staring at moving clouds, we decide to test Buys-Ballot's law. Christoph Buys-Ballot was a Dutch meteorologist who figured out how to locate low-pressure areas by observing the winds, and thereby predict where a storm might be brewing.

We stand with our backs to the wind. According to Buys-Ballot's law, the air pressure on our left will be lower than the air pressure on our right. The wind is blowing from the south in this case, so the area of low pressure is to our left, the west. From that direction a storm will be moving. Great. But then, within seconds, the wind veers, shifts clockwise to come from the west. Does that mean the low pressure is now in the north?

Forget it. We head home, taking a roundabout way past stunted crabapple trees. Their red fruit is ripe and dusty, like Christmas ornaments that need polishing. Our feet mash the fallen crabapples to a golden red pulp.

Hours later, a mackerel sky floats overhead, slightly to the north. I would like a ceiling painted blue and white like this sky. Paint me a cirrocumulus stratiform sky, I'd tell the painter. What? Wave patterns of ice grains, I'd say. The hell? Think of the speckled belly of the trout you caught last Saturday up at Silver Run Creek. Are you nuts? Then I would take him by the hand and show him this northern sky in the late afternoon. Got it.

∽ ∽ ∽

The first snowfall of the year starts one October morning, shortly after dawn. Low clouds hide the mountains and rain drips from the lowered sky, tapping on the golden cottonwood leaves. It's an unfamiliar sound, like the sudden sassy rap of a visiting woodpecker on a cottonwood tree. Then the tapping ends. White scraps of crumbled cloud begin to fall.

At first it is possible to consider each snowflake an individual, to isolate its characteristics as if it were a wildflower in a field guide. The lacy, star-like crystals mark the snowflake type called stellar. The more compact ones with points are known as plates. The ones that look like a clump of gangly roots are spatial dendrites. Other more elongated types are called needles and columns.

Actually these kinds of snowflakes don't all occur in one storm. Their shapes vary depending on the temperature of the mother clouds that spawned them. But soon, as the storm grows and snow falls more heavily, uniqueness becomes an unfathomable concept as it applies to snowflakes. Now all one sees is a white curtain instead of the tiny crystals that form its weave.

Against the backdrop of white land and sky, everyday objects acquire new significance. A car parked on the street, a leaf flattened on the pavement, a telephone wire suspended between house and pole, a tumbleweed in the gutter—the snow redefines each and emphasizes its lines. One sees the curve the car's designers imagined would slip through the wind's fingers. Each vein on the cottonwood leaf stands out. The telephone wire becomes a parabolic curve of silver. The tumbleweed's network of tiny branches looks like a silversmith's sculpture. Even the street looks more meaningful than the small residential street it is; now reduced to black, gray, and white tones, its simple lines echo those of a Japanese block print.

When the sun appears the next day, lines blur, details thicken to mush as the melting begins. Then the wind blows, an eraser of giant proportions. As a former Union Pacific railroader once told me, "Snow doesn't stay around long in southern Wyoming. It just passes through." A day later, Indian summer arrives with strong sunlight and blue skies. Late-turning cottonwoods go yellow overnight.

Years ago, in the late afternoon of Indian summer, my dog and I raced out onto the prairie into that mulled, golden light pouring across the Laramie Valley. We leapt over sagebrush and the low-growing wheels of prickly pear cactus, and tried to outrun the lengthening shadows with a "wind-heeled foot," as Dylan Thomas called it. There was always more land, enough land to contain us so that we never came to an edge where we had to stop. The sun pitched our shadows to their longest, and for a while a twenty-foot-tall girl shadow and a five-foot-tall dog shadow walked with us as our silent companions until the very last moment before sundown. Then the two shadows disappeared into the bunchgrass and red soil, and the two of us turned for home, arriving with the darkening blue of dusk at the back door.

Such a run today, over that stretch of land, would not be possible. New streets score the flattened land. Hundreds of new houses line up side by side. Our house and our street at the edge of town were just part of a greater growth spurt, not the conclusion of it. However, we didn't consider ourselves a link in a chain of development stretching eastward to the Laramie Mountains. We thought we were the last people to build there, and that the space beyond us would be open forever. Instead, when we built at the edge of town, we made it possible for the next house to be built beyond ours, and the next beyond it, and the next, and the next, and the next. Our house did as much to expand the town's limits as the houses that succeeded it.

That is the story of life in the west, from the ancient paleo-Indians to the various Plains tribes to the Spanish to the Anglos. As each new group becomes settled, it begins to consider itself rooted to the place. Then another group arrives, challenges that assumption, and begins to consider itself the rightful occupant until another group comes along to displace it. A contemporary version of this can be witnessed in the clamor heard from Tucson, Arizona north to Missoula, Montana to stop development and to limit growth. Often the loudest voices come from those who have recently moved into the places that were previously open space.

Much as I want to laugh at the hypocrisy and ignorance of those Johnny-come-latelies, I sympathize with them. They, too, lived in or by open space and thought the local settlement would end with their backyards, only to find that their backyards were just the beginning to new settlements.

This is what happened when the edge of town, in our case Laramie, moved past our house. The surveyors came first, men in orange vests, with tripods and wooden stakes topped with orange or yellow or red ribbons. So intent were they on looking through their instruments and measuring the land, I believe they never saw the land they were measuring. In their wake they left wood stakes, stuck into the red dirt in rows that marked the paths of future pipelines, roads, utilities and sewers. My sense of relief at their departure was followed by a burning desire to sneak out and steal the stakes. If one was a child and loved the prairie, one did. If one was an adult and loved the prairie, one did not. Though I was a teenager, I had begun to consider myself an adult. So I did not.

A month later, the big yellow bulldozers and backhoes came and dug two five-foot-deep ditches running for hundreds of yards from north to south. I remember those ditches well, because I could jump down into one and follow it across the prairie, walking at eye level with the grasses, sagebrush, and lichen, out of the wind's reach. My dog hated the ditches, however. When I jumped down and walked northward in the ditch, she walked alone on the prairie above the ditch, looking eye-to-eye at me now and then and whining.

When the bulldozers and scrapers came back several weeks later, they peeled off a layer of prairie—sod, nests, flowers, sagebrush, prickly pear, lichen, rocks—and shoved everything into a big pile. Then they flattened the fine red dirt underneath, and as the wind whipped it into clouds of dust, they dumped a layer of gravel on top, then poured a river of concrete. Lastly, they laid a final suffocating blanket of asphalt over the top. The prairie had disappeared.

The first house they put in was truly a "box made of ticky-tacky," in Pete Seeger's words, with white siding, fake columns, and violent blackish purple brick. Unfortunately, of all the sites the developers could have chosen for this first house in the new development, they picked the lot right behind our house. To add insult to injury, the builder raised the house on a mound of dirt so that now, not more than ten yards from our home, the new house soared upward, so absurdly placed that its basement windows were on the same level as our first-floor windows.

Our neighbors to the north and the south looked at what the builders had done and promptly bought the lots behind their houses so that no abomination could be built there. My parents did what they could, putting in a six-foot-tall fence, buying curtains, and hanging plants to screen the windows. At the time I was upset with them for not trying to buy the land behind our house earlier. But now I see that buying the one lot wouldn't have made any difference. Those two our neighbors bought are now surrounded by houses and streets anyway, and the empty lots look odd, out of place and slightly forlorn. New owners will someday sell the extra land, and houses will eventually appear there too.

Although most people would not lay the blame for the changes that soon occurred to our family on the development of one wild piece of open land,

I feel that it is no coincidence that three years of rapid change suddenly followed. Had my family still had the land on which to roam—the untouched open space beyond our window to absorb our troubles, the sound of meadowlarks and smell of pungent sagebrush just outside our windows to divert our minds—perhaps none of our future family wanderings would have occurred. But in the end, soon after the land was laid over with concrete and houses, we scattered: my parents moved to New York with my brothers, my sister boarded at a friend's house in another part of Laramie, and I found an apartment surrounded by cottonwood trees near the university.

I thought I would stay in Laramie for the rest of my life. I didn't know—who could?—that I would marry young and give birth to three sons in three different towns. I didn't know that I would someday leave Laramie for Fort Collins, then Tucson, Boulder, and Denver. But I would always carry the memory of that first place I'd loved—the prairie behind our house in the Laramie Basin.

Yet after my parents left town, I avoided the neighborhood where I'd grown up. I became a mother of a baby boy and discovered, at nineteen, a whole new world of joys and complications. And of course I found another edge of Laramie from which to explore the land around me, with my baby snuggled in a carrier on my back. But soon my walks devolved to picking my way through the flotsam of construction sites to get to the open land. Here too, development had spread. The edge of the town was changing in all directions. I began to change too. Struggling with the demands of marriage, parenthood, and earning enough money to pay the bills and to eat, I began to think of ways to escape Laramie.

It took several years' worth of recession in the economy, my dropping out of college, my husband Curt's launching of a weekly newspaper and our subsequent financial loss after the newspaper folded, before we finally left. We decided to move to the greener and less windy city of Fort Collins, Colorado, the largest town, at eighty thousand people, within an hour of Laramie, figuring that there the opportunities would be greater.

We cleaned out our apartment and packed a U-Haul trailer to tow behind our fifteen-year-old station wagon. The last thing remaining was an old brown sofa. We had no room to pack it and no one would take it, not even the Salvation Army or Goodwill. We had to leave that day, as our new jobs would start the next day, and we couldn't make two trips as the U-Haul trailer needed to be left in Fort

Collins by a specific time. And the city dump was closed that day.

Desperate to get out of town and begin the new life that awaited us in Fort Collins, Curt and I hauled the sofa out to an abandoned corral northeast of town, where we shoved it out of the station wagon and left it against a fence in a pile of tumbleweeds. We laughed about the old brown sofa with a great view.

But someone saw us and took down our license plate number and called the police. We were escorted back to the corral that afternoon, where the officers watched as we hoisted the sofa back into our station wagon and brought it back to town. We then spent the afternoon looking for another person to take the old thing. That done at last, we emptied the contents of our wallets at City Hall to pay our fine for illegal dumping, then left Laramie, gunning our old station wagon like a rocket out of hell.

I want to laugh at that young woman so desperate to get rid of an old brown sofa, but I can't. How had she changed in those few short years from a child who loved and cherished the land to a woman who opportunistically used it as a dumping ground for an unwanted sofa?

"What would Mrs. Sands have thought of you if she had heard what you did?" I imagined someone asking. "To think that you passed yourself off as some-one who cared about the environment when you really didn't care at all."

But Mrs. Sands was dead, would come my answer. I was pregnant again, the mother of a toddler; my husband could only find a low-paying job report-ing on high school sports for a daily newspaper, and we were deeply in debt at the ripe old ages of twenty-one and twenty-two. All I cared about was finding a secure income, an end to collection agency letters, and a way to pay for the birth of this second child, as we had no health insurance. The prairie would have to manage without me.

As I saw it, the only difference between me and the developers who had ruined the prairie behind our house was that I had been fined for dumping and the developers had been paid. I fled Laramie empty-handed, but they left with fat wallets.

A few times each year I returned to Laramie to visit my husband's family, but never to the side of town where I'd been raised. Years later, however, curiosity won out over the sadness I'd felt at seeing the prairie disappear under asphalt and concrete, and I decided to go see what trace, if any, was left of my spe-cial place out on the prairie, my circle of rock walls and stone ledges.

I navigated as my husband drove us past row after row of semi-identical houses, all variations on three tedious floor plans. It seemed as though an entire town had been built behind my old house. Soon I lost my bearings and couldn't say with any certainty where I'd walked and played as a child. I looked for the old pale green house of the rancher, Mr. Lamb, who'd lived a good long walk from our house, but I couldn't even find that. As we wandered up one street and down the next, I wondered if his house had been torn down. About to give up, we rounded a corner and saw it. Still painted green, it was surrounded by new houses. Where the outbuildings had been, and a dirt road, and barbed wire fencing, the developers had stuck a small park with a buck rail fence, green sod, and skinny ponderosa pine saplings held upright by wires and stakes.

We stopped and got out. The wind whipped across the land as it always had. Since the ranch house was here, I reasoned, my stone circle must lie to the west and north, through this backyard, over that hill, across this little cul-de-sac—but no. Just more houses and yards and streets slapped onto the land. I searched for a way to translate my mental map of the prairie into the reality of the subdivision, a way to superimpose one over the other like layers of cellophane. Then at least I could fix on someone's backyard and say with certainty, "My stone circle used to be over there." But there was no translation. No way to even guess where my special place had been. It had disappeared.

So began the separation in my mind between the mythic land of my childhood and the territory of my adulthood. The mythic land was a place un-bounded, full of abundance for the senses, open to all who loved it and could move lightly over it. As an adult, I live on real estate, a commodity that can be sold and completely altered to suit the whims of human desires.

The mythic land was that blank space on the old maps of the Laramie Basin, stretching from the old city limits at around 7,200 feet to Pilot Knob, the 9,000-foot-high point ten miles to the east. Within that mythic land lay simple beauty and mystery. Evening primrose and sego lily grew, and scarlet mallow, and purple harebells. Buffalo grass, needle grass, and hairy grama grass held the red dirt in with their networks of roots, and sagebrush and great round colonies of prickly pear studded the land with texture. Meadowlarks flew up from hidden nests in a streak of yellow to perch on the tallest sagebrush and pour their liquid songs. Here a narrow path threaded through sagebrush three feet high, there the traces of old wagon ruts cut lightly into the red dirt. Here the land rose slightly, there it dipped. Never flat. Never empty.

If I had that map today, I would take my paints and mix them to just the right orange-pink color of the dirt after a rainstorm and spread it where we used to roam, then take some Mars black and feather a line of barbed wire along the top edge. Nasim could identify each type of barbed wire fence by name and by date manufactured, just by looking at the particular twist of wire and the way the thorn-like barb was attached, but to me, wire was wire, sharp and unpleasant. Then I would mix some yellow ocher with a little cadmium red and stroke in the tumbled sandstone blocks we used to scramble over, the ruins, we always thought, of some pioneer's house. North of that, I'd scumble in the red hills sparsely covered in bunchgrass where the sheep ran like water in the summer. To the east and slightly south, a myriad of warm neutrals in pink, gold, and lavender would mark my special place, the circle of stones. Perhaps I'd dot in purple and gold the mounds of flowers that covered the floor of the circle. The narrow path back home, an old cow trail, would appear as a thin burnt umber line.

That is how the map would look, the map of the place I loved. A different map of the place can be found in the Laramie telephone book. It is a map of the real and the profane, consisting of lines imposed on the land with no care taken to orient them to the sun or the wind, with a grid of oddly named streets, so their residents won't forget, in their blinding numbness to the identical houses, where it is they live.

The names of these streets are taken from people and things long since decimated or destroyed by the dominant culture—mine. Names of Native American tribes and chiefs. Names of the nearly-extinct plants and flowers that the houses and yards displaced. Names that try to hide the fact that these houses and streets are ugly. Names that try to establish the right of these new residents to live here, appropriating the images of the area's natural history. It sounds beautiful: Indian Paintbrush Drive. Named for the state flower. Can one find a trace of that wildflower on that street? Of course not.

Nothing but siding, asphalt, concrete, and green sod slapped together so carelessly that it doesn't even approach manmade beauty, let alone natural beauty. The land has become a receptacle for something far worse, a far more systematic betrayal, than a brown sofa abandoned beside an old corral.

∿ ∿ ∿

Sundown. The winds have stilled and the sudden quiet draws people from their homes into that intense light during the half-hour before sunset. The red hills and the golden grasses seem to give off their own stored light. Every gully, every outcropping, every path is visible in this light; every stem of dried grass, every thorn of Russian thistle, casts its own long shadow. Texture is everywhere and the eyes feast on the sight. This is why we live here: for the moment when the winds still and the light gives everything it touches grace and beauty.

Maybe only a child could have loved the land I loved. I take no comfort in thinking that maybe another child is out there roaming the prairie with a dog this evening, a child who lives on one of those numb little streets named after a displaced Indian tribe. Maybe that child's favorite places will last as long as twenty years, long enough to be shared with his or her children perhaps. Maybe not.

The long arm of the Medicine Bow Range darkens to dusky blue on the other side of the valley. The Arapaho gathered wood in those mountains to make bows and arrows for hunting. Perhaps the wood was "good medicine," making strong bows for the hunters who killed game for the tribe. But there's more to it than that. These mountains, and the valley beneath them, are good medicine for people today, members of the post-nuclear age tribe, hungry for more than meat, needing beauty and solitude more than venison. The valley quiets as darkness comes. The wind rises, then dies. A hunter's moon glows in the silence, a pale yellow leaf in the branches of the night sky. On the horizon it looks bigger and rounder than it really is, an optical illusion I willingly accept as real.

I decide to continue my search for my special place another day. If it turns out to be under someone's garage or buried by their driveway, at least I'll have a grave to mourn by, to decorate with flowers and surveyor's stakes.

The wind comes up again. Raised by the moon, Nasim would say. Although the doors and windows are shut, the wind finds a place to put its mouth to the house. It moans in the chimney and puffs the curtains. Gentle as a moth's tongue, it presses fine red dust into the smallest openings, leaving thread-like lines on sills and thresholds. Outside, it hisses in the grass, reminding me of the rustle of dried leaves, or the sound of olive oil as it is poured into a hot frying pan, or rain falling lightly on stones. Trying to blow the moon down, it fails, and howls in disappointment. Should the wind ever reach the moon, surely it would be because the world had ended. The final blast that would touch that lifeless, gray place would carry the red dust of southern Wyoming among the ashes of all the world's living creatures.

Let the wind blow.

WHITE LOCUST WIND

Early winter

DRIVING THROUGH A blizzard can easily erase one's mental maps of a road and its landscape. At once all traces of the familiar disappear in the blinding snowfall and suddenly the countryside seems alien.

Heading from our new home in Boulder to visit Curt's family in Laramie one afternoon, we notice snow beginning to fall. I argue for turning back. Curt argues for pushing on. I let him win, feeling more reassured by his confidence than by the fields slowly fading into mist around us. Cottonwoods stand out in the veils of falling snowflakes, huge, implacable guardians, their dark gray branches impossibly forked, each pattern of limb and branch like no other. These aren't young saplings new to unfiltered sunlight and pushy winds. In fact, there aren't any young trees around these fields at all. Where are the replacements growing? When each tree turns white and leafless, will it break apart into the earth with no young one to take its place?

Contemplating the lack of young cottonwoods takes my mind off the growing snowstorm for a few miles or so. Then, as the early winter twilight droops into night, we head northwest out of Fort Collins, the northernmost city in Colorado's Front Range corridor. Up into the folds of the foothills we drive, where lonely lights from distant houses sparkle for a moment, then disappear as the car moves on. In the darkness, as snow whips before our headlights, I feel dizzy looking out the window. On a road as familiar to me as my driveway, I suddenly feel lost. Have we reached Owl Canyon? Or have we already passed it, and the Forks and Steamboat Rock? How long ago? Time loses all boundaries without the borders of land and sky and light to guide us. We are like two lost pilots flying blind, but instead of relying on instruments to navigate, we must follow this snowy ribbon of road to take us where we want to go.

At night in the falling snow, the landscape becomes a landscape of the mind. This dark mass to the right, felt but not seen, could be Red Mountain, a monolith of red rock. The hill the car rushes down could be the little valley of Dale Creek. Yet a small voice tells me I'm making up my surroundings and in reality we're miles from anywhere familiar. Worse, what if the car should break down here, in the middle of this snowstorm, in this swirling darkness?

At least we'd be *somewhere*. The idea, however, is to just keep moving at all costs: in movement lies salvation. Follow the gray rope of the road just as the Plains farmers follow the clothesline tied between house and barn during blizzards. Let go of the rope and wander blindly. Stay with the rope and at its end is light, warmth, and a hot dinner.

∾ ∾ ∾

Ordinarily this is my favorite road, this section of Highway 287 between Fort Collins and Laramie. It's not straight-arrow boring, nor is it the kind of elevated highway one finds in Colorado's Glenwood Canyon or the Blue Ridge Mountains back east. Such a highway, floating above the land on stilts, tries as little as possible to intrude on the riverbank or forests below. But 287 doesn't float— it snuggles down, tight as a zipper. Sometimes it even digs into the flesh of the land, when it cuts through the hogbacks near Owl Canyon, leaving high walls of red sandstone which stick out like wounds.

Long before this highway was built, the Overland Trail ran between Fort Collins and Laramie. The Overland Trail was established in 1862 as a stage-coach route over an earlier 1850 wagon road called the Cherokee Trail when Indian uprisings further north on the Oregon Trail made travel there difficult. An estimated twenty thousand people used the Overland Trail as a route to new lives in the west. Paralleling it and sometimes overlapping it, today's highway weaves in and out of the hills and valleys of northern Colorado on its way to the high plains of southern Wyoming.

Every time I drive it, I see something new: an outcropping of rosy sandstone, the sun washing over the short grass of the high prairie near Phantom Canyon, a small pool sparkling blue-black at the bottom of a narrow gorge, wagon ruts carved into a rocky slab of hillside. My husband's father, a Laramie resident, first drove this stretch of highway over forty years ago. He has driven it well over a thousand times since then, in all kinds of weather, at all times of day and night. Once, near the state line, he saw a distant ranch house, one he'd never seen before. The next time he drove back through, he made a point of looking for the ranch house. He couldn't find it and hasn't seen it since.

As a child I divided this highway into segments, to make the trip seem shorter. The first segment on the way home to Laramie whispers past ranchettes just northwest of Fort Collins, where 287 follows the Cache la Poudre River upstream into a small green foothills valley. River and highway separate at Ted's Place, the site of several restaurant incarnations and now a generic chain gas station. When I was young I imagined my grandfather had named the place, as his name, too, was Ted. After Ted's Place, the highway narrows and passes through the blizzard gates. This is the point where city lights disappear and starlight reigns. After this gate, there are no more towns for over fifty miles. I used to think of it as the point of no return.

In the next segment, the road shoots north beneath a high ridge of limestone blocks, many of which lie at the base of the ridge, having tumbled eons ago. On the other side of the road, a long red hogback of Dakota sandstone rises two stories high. An Overland Trail stagecoach station once lay behind this hill. Abandoned, and later taken over by the Musgrove gang of horse thieves around 1868, the station provided the perfect hideout from which to prey on wagon trains and ranchers. Now it's a hideaway for landowners escaping the suburban sprawl of Fort Collins.

Cutting west through dark orange sandstone cliffs, the highway hooks northward and barrels along the base of a piñon-pine-studded hill. As the highway slides down into a scoop of land, it crosses the Overland Trail at the Forks, a café marking the turnoff to the Red Feather Lakes. Built in 1874, the original two-story building burned down in 1985, but was rebuilt to look like its predecessor.

Here we turned south one summer day to search for Curt's grandfather's childhood home. Our only clue was an old photograph, taken around 1915, of Curt's great-aunt and her friend. The two girls wear sunbonnets and pretend to hang off the edge of a precipice. Bare mountains ring the scene, and behind the girls stretches a deep valley with a thread of dark trees in the distance below. On the back of the photograph someone wrote: "The ranch house is located where the trees are in the background behind the girls." It is my husband's only photograph of the ranch. A fire destroyed the barns and house in the 1920s and family legend tells that it also incinerated the family fortune, rumored to have been hidden in coffee cans in the ranch house.

We drove all over that valley that day, squinting at the photograph and comparing it to the terrain around us. Maybe the ranch had been over there—a creek running by would account for the trees growing in the photograph. But look again: in the photograph, a mountain rises to the west of the creek; here it's to the north. This is not the place.

We never found it. Now and then someone in the family mentions the ranch, but no one feels a need to keep searching. We are all city dwellers and the ranch has been relegated to the mists and myth of family history.

Now, north of the Forks, the highway crosses a culvert that funnels water into an underground channel, then turns and heads up a ridge. Across the valley to the west, the snow-spackled peaks of the Rocky Mountains float like a movie set backdrop, larger than life. Across the valley to the east, a sandstone formation juts from the bony backbone of the earth: Steamboat Rock and its tugboat to south. In the long grass closer to the highway, cattle graze near the ruts of the Overland Trail. Now the highway flattens as it zips across the high plains near Phantom Canyon and Red Mountain and the semi trucks make up for time lost on the winding road. And then, like a great exhalation, comes the quick descent into a grassy valley of hay meadows. Here the little community church of Virginia Dale perches by the road, its white siding wind-scoured, its tiny graveyard windblown and lonely.

Up the hill to the old café and post office labeled Virginia Dale. The old stagecoach station still stands nearby on private land, functioning even into the 1940s as a general store. Back in the early 1860s, when stagecoaches rumbled by with passengers and mail, the Virginia Dale stage stop was known as a well-stocked oasis, where humans and animals found plenty to eat and drink. Run by Jack Slade, whose name usually is preceded by "the notorious," the place was named for his wife, Virginia. Much has been written about Jack Slade's escapades: he was known to get drunk and shoot up saloons, and it was commonly believed that the stage robbers in the area were in cahoots with him. When masked bandits held up a stagecoach in 1863 and took a gold shipment worth sixty thousand dollars, Slade was fired from the stagecoach station. He and Virginia soon left the area for Virginia City, Montana. None of the gold was ever recovered, though the bandits were hunted down and killed. Many presume Jack Slade took the gold with him or hid it well in the boulder-strewn hills.

I had always assumed that his wife Virginia was a retiring thing, sweet and docile, overwhelmed by her rough husband. Certainly we never learned about Virginia in school, though we were given the cleaned-up version of Jack. I doubt that Nasim knew about

Virginia Slade, though I think Nasim would have liked her story.

Virginia was, pound for pound, the perfect match for Jack. Rumored to have been a prostitute in her pre-Slade years, Virginia was as strong-willed as she was voluptuous. When vigilantes hanged Slade in Montana, she rode into town on her horse and confronted the crowd. Threatened with her own imminent hanging, she grabbed Slade's body and took it back to her ranch where she pickled it in a metal coffin and kept it under her bed until she could take it to Salt Lake City for burial. After that task was accomplished, she married again, divorced, then married yet again, all the while trying to regain rights to the Montana ranch that Slade had owned. She never returned to northern Colorado, spending her final years in Missouri. Recently her namesake town in Colorado became the home of an order of nuns who sought peace and quiet away from the Denver metro area. They built a large chapel and compound nearby, which one can glimpse from the highway. Perhaps Virginia's ghost visits the place, bemused.

Northeast of Virginia Dale, Dale Creek worms its way between huge cliffs of pink Sherman granite. In the late 1860s when the Union Pacific railroad came through Wyoming, Dale Creek and its canyon walls were in the way. Railroad crews built a wooden trestle across the creek, linking the two high cliffs. It was the longest wooden trestle of its time. Old photographs show a structure that seems to be made of thousands of toothpicks. However, closer inspection of the photograph reveals the true scale when one sees how tiny the men standing on top of the trestle appear. Each "toothpick" must have been over twelve feet long.

Was the trestle still there? Nasim and I had intended to search, but never got around to it. One hot August morning years later my husband, my brother, and I walked out from the Ames Monument, a sandstone pyramid constructed to honor the Ames brothers who were instrumental in building this section of the railroad, to see what we could find of the trestle. Nearby we saw the faint outlines on the green meadow grass of the old railroad camp of Sherman, once a bustling place with a store, stables, and blacksmith shop. We hiked along the old railroad bed for miles as the sun rose and a silver horizon began to ripple with heat waves. The smell of old creosote-soaked wooden ties pinched our noses and mingled with the scent of the huge sagebrush that seemed to grow larger the farther we walked. At last we reached the cliff, high above Dale Creek. Pilings still clung to the rock's edge where they had been bolted into the granite, but all other traces of the immense wooden structure had vanished.

Past Virginia Dale and Dale Creek, the highway rises again. Here and there it seems as though the ponderosa pines are growing right out of the pink granite boulders. Northeast of this area, on Interstate 80 between Cheyenne and Laramie, one boulder is fenced and adorned with a plaque as a curiosity for tourists. They stand and wonder, how did that tree grow out of that rock? The answer is, from simple forces, persistently applied. Wind and rain carved the granite, grain by grain, coupled with the slow yet tenacious embrace of lichen, creating small pockets of soil. In these pockets, windblown seeds find a bare minimum of nutrients and just enough protection from the elements. Years ago, a pine seedling must have landed from a gust of wind and taken hold in a niche in this rock before the interstate was even built. Actually, a pine tree growing on a boulder is no rare occurrence but such a sight does deserve a stop, simply to pay homage to the life force at work.

Continuing north from Virginia Dale, the road rides the swells and dips of pine and rock-studded hills. At night in spring and fall deer sometimes brave the asphalt, cross in front of oncoming cars, then suddenly halt, blinded by headlights in mid-stride. One particular spring night we saw four separate accident scenes involving deer on this stretch; the red-streaked pavement and inert brown forms by the side of the road testified to each. We learned to watch the roadside for the telltale sparkle of headlights glancing off deer eyes, slowing down immediately just in case the deer tried to bolt; still, the squeal of our brakes announced several near misses.

At the Wyoming state line, a store and sign proclaim the new jurisdiction. Nature's own borderline is more sharply drawn just north: pine forest abruptly stops and naked land begins. Summers these treeless hills wear only a skin of grass, winters a thin armor of polished snow. This is the highest ground, the summit. Up here, the wind rules, turning over semi trucks, throwing sheets of blinding snow, flinging tumbleweeds for miles. Nothing grows taller than ankle level here.

However, beneath its prickly surface, the earth nurtures treasures: diamonds discovered in the area years ago. Hearing of them as a fourteen-year-old I imagined white jewels as large as ostrich eggs nestled in layers of rocky soil. Unfortunately, or fortunately, depending on one's point of view, the diamonds are small and mining them has proved expensive. Only a few have tried, and with little success until recently. Fortunate, because the land doesn't heal quickly here in the west where sun and wind erode the soil steadily. One conical hill near the highway was dynamited open more than two decades ago and the inside gutted for diamonds or other treasures. But it looks as though it was blown up only yesterday. Huge stones lie where they must have been been thrown by the dynamite. Bare red dirt scabs the ragged edge of the hole where the top of the hill was sheared off.

Before dynamite, before humans, kimberlite exploded upwards here in southern Wyoming from deep in the earth's mantle, forming pipes of hot magma that flowed along fractures in the earth's crust. Small craters pocked the surface, beneath which, lining the cooled magma, lay the kimberlite diamonds.

Nasim was not one to wear diamonds. Too cold-looking, she said. But I think she would have appreciated the human-created diamonds an engineer once dropped into the palm of my hand for me to examine. He was showing me the fruit of the diamond anvil, a powerful device created by university scientists to manufacture diamonds for industrial use. These little grayish minerals in my hand seemed a far sight from the glittering white diamonds of the jeweler's trade, but I'll bet Nasim would have been more interested in these rough rocks and their practical uses. Maybe she would have even asked, as I did not, to keep one.

∾ ∾ ∾

Now the storm continues to blow as our headlights tangle with snowflakes and winds jiggle the car in the dark. We are crossing a great bare place. Even in this blizzard, it's easy to tell we have reached the summit. These next five miles of open mountaintop are the most dangerous: trucks jackknife on this section of highway even in clear weather, and the sunniest day masks brutal gusts that can wrench the steering wheel from a driver's hands. Our headlights push uselessly against the darkness, illuminating the simple fact that we are caught in a full-scale blizzard. It's likely that even now the blizzard gates are closing back at Ted's Place and the highway patrol is turning travelers back. Push on, push on.

In this curtain of snow the edge of the highway merges with the prairie. Slowly we crawl from blizzard pole to blizzard pole, these three-foot high metal sticks our only confirmation that we are still even on the highway. Suddenly the front end of the car slopes downward. We begin the descent into the Laramie Basin. The lights of Laramie, twenty miles away, are usually visible, but tonight we see nothing but the white of the snow in our headlights, like billions of white locusts beating their wings against our progress. If it weren't for the pull of gravity drawing us down the hill, we wouldn't even know we were descending.

We had told family members to expect us in under three hours. Otherwise, come looking for us, we joked on the phone before leaving. The snowflakes had floated down light and harmless as ashes, melting as they touched the house and street, and a blizzard seemed only a paranoid imagining. Now, after four hours on the road, we roll slowly in first gear down the summit, and crawl past Tie Siding, once a lumbering area and source of ties for the railroad. Crews floated thousands of logs down the Laramie River to the tie plant at Laramie. Tonight Tie Siding's few rooftops are barely discernible in the snow.

We lumber across the dark land. Finally the cement plant's lights welcome us, and we top an overpass above the railroad tracks and glide down into town. Streetlights glow around us like fuzzy white dandelions gone to seed, and the snow sparkles merrily in the light. Suddenly a familiar-looking car honks as it passes us and turns down our street.

The family had taken us at our word. When we didn't show up, they had gone out looking for us, but in the confusion of blowing snow we hadn't noticed them on the highway. Luckily they had recognized our car, turned around, and tailed us home.

Much has been said and written about the rugged individualism of the west, the cowboy being the prime exemplar. But this storm reminds us would-be individualists of the necessity for bonds among us, even if it's just one person following another to make sure he gets home.

Coyote Wind

Winter

IN WINTER THE coyote wind howls. Such a restless wind. It brushes every cottonwood branch, then rolls among the pale dry tops of the buffalo grass before trotting off to whip a windchime or two.

A whirl of fine snowflakes rises in the sunshine, as if a child's plastic snow globe had just been shaken. Sheltered from the wind by the bulk of the house, I observe the wind without feeling its bite. The coyote wind is true to its name. It cries at the corners of the house, singing its mournful song. It noses where it shouldn't, tips over trash cans and opens gates, eats poodles and sheep and stray cats.

The ancient Irish had names for eight winds, all of which show a Roman influence and many much more fearsome than my coyote wind. Solanus produced plague and disease; favonius, puinina, pessima, and faiccina, blowing from various directions, were also ill winds that brought no good. Altanus, though an ill wind, also brought fish beneath it in the ocean currents; africus, from the southeast, brought good harvest of the earth and sea, and savonicus, a south wind, brought larger-than-usual fish.

Nasim told me that the Irish also assigned colors to the winds. The north wind, for instance, was a black wind. The south wind was white. A wind from the east would be purple; from the southeast, red or yellow. Northwesterly winds were dark brown or gray, southwesterly winds green or grayish green. Three winds more difficult to visualize are the dark wind from the east-northeast, the speckled wind from the north-northeast, and the pale wind from the west. Years later, I recalled Nasim's story when I read in Flann O'Brien's contemporary Irish novel of a character who believes that the winds have colors and that the wind blowing at the time of one's birth imparts its color to the newborn. Hence the character, born during an east-southeasterly wind, believes that he has a yellow hue, which darkens as he grows older. When the yellow darkens to black, he will die.

Poor coyote wind. It only brings flurries of white, and cold temperatures. It inspires a certain energy found only at the beginning of winter, before the mind has become weary of cold. True, the coyote wind hounds and pesters. It whines, "Go inside. Get out of my territory." It stubs the dirt and throws it into my eyes, then ruffles my dog's fur and disappears. For a moment, calm. Relief from the low roar of molecules flowing past. Maybe it has run down to Tie Siding, or over the range to Cheyenne. Then a large sagebrush shivers. My scarf suddenly unwinds. The coyote wind trots over—"Are you leaving yet?"

But now I walk deeper into its territory, away from the protection of house and trees. Here, on the prairie's thin white crust, the top layer of powdered snow circles endlessly in the wind like an eddy in a stream. Pushing with full strength from the west, the wind blows away the thin layer of warm air surrounding my body. Prairie dwellers knew about wind-chill factor long before it had a name. When wind and chill combine, the effect is much colder than the mere temperature shown on a thermometer. For instance, if the wind is blowing at just a soft ten miles per hour on a zero-degree morning, the coldness one's body feels out in that wind is not zero but twenty-two degrees below.

The white crust of snow ends abruptly and Spring Creek appears at the same instant I hear its businesslike clatter over the rocky streambed. It seems odd to see this creek gurgle along, wet and alive, in this semi-arid country where the wind and the earth greedily suck up any moisture that the sun hasn't evaporated first.

I saw a ponderosa pine die one year in a particularly windy, dry corner of Laramie. In late summer it was still green, standing about five feet tall. By autumn its needles had turned brown at the tips. Winter winds did little to help, blowing away much of the snow before it could melt and drip into the soil. After one blizzard, the sun came out and the snow-covered branches of the tree began to glisten. One could practically see the tree drinking in the snowmelt. Then the wind came. Branches seemed to smolder with thick clouds of smoke as the snow blew off, sprinkling the air with millions of fragments of light. Soon the tree was bare, the needles dry again. By spring it had turned reddish brown, just when the thick sod of the short plains grass was coming back to life, just when a few rain showers kited across the valley, and tiny crocuses appeared like yellow and purple drops in the moist soil. The tree let go its needles and died.

∽ ∽ ∽

Southeastern Wyoming receives between fourteen and sixteen inches of moisture per year, which puts it in the category of semi-arid region, bordering on desert. Native plants adapt by wearing light colors such as gray green, silver green, and blue gray to reflect the sun's rays and reduce the loss of water from their leaves.

The explorer Stephen Long called the west the "Great American Desert." An unfortunate choice of words, it reflected not so much the characteristics of the land as his own prejudices and background. Long was from the east and brought with him his own region's notions of beauty, utility, and normality. Of course it seemed like a desert to him, coming from a wetter climate. But what if he had recently arrived from the outback of Australia, or closer to here, Death Valley? The word "jungle," of course, still would not have fit the west, but in his eyes neither would have the word "desert."

When we left Fort Collins for Tucson in southern Arizona to live in the desert, I asked simply that it make its mark on me. Coming from the dry plains of Wyoming and the parched foothills of the Rocky Mountains, I was prepared for water rationing at the least. But when we passed through Phoenix, two hours to the north of our destination, on a sunny 112-degree afternoon in August, sprinklers were watering the grass and concrete on the medians of Interstate 10.

My offer of sacrifice had just been rejected.

This is the challenge that many of us alternately seek and dodge: to live within our means. Not just economically, but environmentally. It is not easy to find poetry in living within limits and I have failed the challenge many times. Still, I seek it.

I see people moving into subdivisions across the west, where developers have promoted not just the pretty views but the easy access to wildlife nearby. After a few garden bushes disappear into the mouths of browsing deer, and a few cats and poodles disappear into the mouths of browsing coyotes and mountain lions, the wildlife lovers demand the removal of the offending beasts. Why not just accept the restrictions of life in that environment and forgo such favorite bushes, forgo a garden altogether, and certainly forgo cats and dogs if one finds it objectionable that they may join the food chain. But no. We want it all. We accept no restrictions.

Instead we trap the wild animals because they eat the pets we shouldn't have brought with us. We irrigate the desert so that it will look like the lawns we left behind in wetter climates. We flatten the rolling landscape to save the developers the expense of building on contours. We dam the river because it floods once a year or once a century. We drain the marsh because land that cannot be built on or planted does not turn a profit and therefore is not valuable.

The black-and-white issues are easy: it's wrong to litter the land, whether with a sofa or with urban blight; it's wrong to let single-hulled oil tankers cruise near rocky coasts; it's wrong to dump raw sewage and poisonous chemicals into rivers our downstream neighbors drink from. It's the little details, the daily trade-offs, that become tough to figure. Save electricity and write longhand on paper? Or save paper and revise on the computer? Use cloth diapers and save the landfills from overflowing? Or use disposable diapers and save water and energy? So begins a series of compromises: I'll drive to work, but in a car that gets good gas mileage. I'll use plastic and glass bottles, but I'll recycle them. I'll use a clothes dryer in the winter but dry my sheets outside on the clothesline in summer.

Nasim!

"It's not as though we're some invader species," she told me once as we tramped beside soggy willow bushes near Tie Siding, south of Laramie. I had become so concerned about even such common practices as wearing bug spray to ward off insects that I guess she probably realized she had to provide some balance. "We are born and made of this planet, hon. We're made of calcium, like seashells, and iron, like rocks. We've got saltwater from the ocean in our blood and nitrogen from the soil in our bodies. Don't you see? Our bodies hold clues that tie us to this planet. The moon and the tides affect a woman's menstrual period. The air pressure and the wind affect men's and women's moods. Our mistake is in thinking that we can and should control everything." She stopped talking to catch her breath and wiped a freckled hand across her forehead.

"The way I see it," she said, swinging her arms and stomping along through the mushy hay beside the willow bushes, "Is that we should go back to the idea of kin. We are the planet's cousin and we are cousin to everything on it." She had wanted to find a kind of frog that lived in the stream near the willow bushes, but as often happened, our conversation drove away the wild thing we were hoping to see. Ah well. She raised her shoulders and rolled her eyes. We sat down to rest on some large rocks beside the stream and she took out the water bottle from her backpack and peeled an orange to share. Then she told me about her husband, Robert, and the time—just before he was diagnosed with Parkinson's—when he encountered a coyote.

Robert liked to go out with a rifle during deer-hunting season, though this didn't make him a hunter.

He rarely shot anything and hunting season was just an excuse to tramp around outside. One day he was walking a ridge where he knew he'd have a good chance of seeing deer and an even better chance of seeing coyotes. Sure enough, one soon trotted into view below him. The coyote was moving near the bottom of the ridge while Robert stayed just over its crest so he could peer over now and then as he followed the coyote without being seen.

The coyote seemed to grow nervous. The wind was blowing away from it, so Robert knew he hadn't been scented. But still the coyote kept stopping and looking around as if it knew it was being followed. Finally Robert decided to let the coyote see him. He stood up near the crest of the ridge so that he was partly outlined against the sky. When the coyote looked at him, Robert just stood there.

The coyote nonchalantly went back to its hunting, then suddenly stopped again and glanced back at Robert as if hoping to catch him off guard. Several times the coyote did this, but each time Robert stood still. Then the coyote gave up all pretense and stared at him up on the ridge. Suddenly it barked at him, as if to ask, "Who the hell are you?"

Robert slowly stepped to the crest of the ridge and stood in full view, trembling slightly, a symptom of the Parkinson's, though he didn't know it at the time. The coyote studied him up and down, then turned and continued on its way.

Native American stories, too, remind their listeners of the connections between humans and their environment. People are formed of earth or wind or mud, or shift from human to animal shape as quick as a thought. When the coyote wind blows and I feel I don't belong out here, I think of an Apache story of the creation of humans, as told by Joseph Campbell. The birds and animals wanted a companion, so they went to their creator, who sent them on an extended scavenger hunt for a variety of objects. They gathered opal and turquoise, jet, abalone, yellow pollen, and red clay, and brought this motley collection to their creator. Using the pollen, the creator drew an outline on the ground of a figure, which was then filled in with the beautiful stones: opal for the fingernails, jet for the eyes, turquoise for the veins, and so on, until the human was nearly complete. A nearby rain cloud crowned the new being with a head of hair. To breathe life into this being, the creator made the wind blow into the shape that had been outlined on the ground. We can still see the wind's print on the whorls of our fingertips. They trace the path the wind took at our creation, and when the spirit leaves the body at death, its path will follow the print of the whorls on the soles of our feet.

On this bitter, windy day, I look at my cold, red fingers and remember this story as I stand on a footbridge spanning Spring Creek. The wind picks up, or was it always there? Above the tumble of the water comes a faint humming sound, which then slips higher into a clear note. I look around, puzzled, but I'm alone. The note plays again. Then another resonates, lower in tone, like panpipes. Who is this invisible musician? Am I hearing things? I stand, confused. Then a faint vibration passes through the bridge's tubular railing to my hands. It's the bridge. The wind has shifted just right, catching the pipe railings and blowing them like a pipe organ. Notes fly around me as I shiver and listen.

"Honey," Nasim would say, "Just do what you can. Don't waste what you've been given, whether it's food or water or paper or glass or some earth or an education or a gift from God. Just do what you can with what you've got."

I do belong out here on this cold bridge above the creek. The wind that plays the pipe railings on the bridge is the same wind that moves through my mouth to play the flute. The rocks the water flows over are the color of my eyes. The calcium of the snail's shell structures my bones as well. Hair of golden-brown grama grass, skin of yellow pollen, blood of scarlet mallow, I belong. I belong.

SKIPPING STONE WIND

Winter suspended

SOLSTICE. THE calendar and the sun's position in the sky say that winter begins in earnest today, but the skipping stone wind skitters across the prairie, bringing a day of warmth to melt the snow down to bare brown grass again. By the time of the winter solstice, the body and spirit cling to the memory of long sunlit days and try to survive through brief daylight and long night. Just when it seems each night will stretch longer and longer until darkness conquers all, suddenly the stretching stops. The solstice shifts the balance back. Minds accustomed to pessimism caused by the lack of daylight now pivot hopefully in the direction of summer, as pessimism turns to optimism. Yes, the days *will* grow longer, the nights *will* shrink, minute by minute, starting after this day: the winter solstice has come.

My husband, children, and I are driving northwest across the huge open floor of the basin, bound for California to spend a few days there. The sky stretches above us like a great blue parachute. Speckled brown and white, the Laramie Basin's colors have been lifted from a sparrow's breast. Snow flocks the dirt where there is no vegetation. To the north, the plains appear more pinkish brown, and at the horizon, Laramie Peak shimmers like a blue mirage. The peak was a major landmark to pioneers, one they could look forward to spotting, the signal that their journey was about halfway through. To them, this distant blue pyramid was a symbol of hope that journey's end would indeed be reached, whereas for me, it's a lovely image to weave into memory. It seems I'm more conscious of the beauty of this place when I am leaving it for somewhere else.

What did those men and women pioneers think as they traveled this route west at the pace of a plodding ox? Did they grow to enjoy some aspects— the blue sky, the fresh wind, the pungent-smelling sagebrush, the strong sunshine—or did the slow pace and memories of more lush landscapes make them hate every step? And later, when travelers covered this route by stagecoach, were they grateful for a fleet-footed team of horses or more interested in the expansive views?

Obviously most saw this part of the west as a country to pass through, not as a destination. How did that attitude affect the land and later settlers? How do people perceive a land that others wanted to traverse quickly, thinking only of the lands behind them and ahead of them? Well, how do most people perceive an object that others have discarded or found wanting? How do most people behave when tunnel vision blinds them to the beauty around them? If I could litter the land with a sofa of an unbecoming shade of brown, land I had once loved and cherished, in my hurry to get out of town, then why am I surprised and irritated at the occupants of homes south of Laramie, some with beautiful views of snowy peaks, whose junked cars stud the prairie? At least those early travelers who thought of southeastern Wyoming as a wasteland hurried through without doing prolonged damage to the land. Those of us who stay sometimes find that our presence hurts the land worse.

But then again, I am an expert at making mountains out of clouds. I didn't choose to live here, but after a while I came to feel that the land had chosen me. I was someone who could love it, prickles, wind, dust, and all. After all, I knew even at the age of five that Iowa was not the place for me. Playing by the

Skunk River, away from the claustrophobia-inducing woods so I could see open sky, I would pretend the clouds I saw on the horizon were mountains. Massive, round, bleached white peaks towered above Ames like the brothers and sisters of Mount Everest. Sometimes I almost believed my own imagination.

Later, when we moved to Wyoming and I discovered my father's old German Leica rangefinder camera, I didn't shoot pictures of mountains, even though we were surrounded by them. Instead, I aimed my lens at the constantly changing sky and the wide-open plains of the Laramie Basin. My parents were flabbergasted when they saw the results. "They are clouds. Just clouds. Why would you want to photograph clouds?" I remember my father saying as he looked at a shot of a lacy white cirrus cloud sailing in a sea of blue. The next photograph was its brother, the next its mother, and so on, a family album of cirrus clouds.

"They're not all clouds," I said. I showed him the photographs of the prairie, a curve of golden brown rising gently behind our house like the back of some ancient dinosaur, but I couldn't answer his question. Why I found the sky and the prairie beautiful, I didn't know. I just knew they were special.

The land was shaping my idea of beauty, whereas my parents arrived with their conception of beauty already formed. My Wyoming was not the same as theirs. Their Wyoming was Colter Bay and Jenny Lake at the foot of the Grand Tetons, and Yellowstone Canyon and the Wind River Range. My Wyoming was a small intermountain grassland basin walled by pre-Cambrian granitic mountains to the east and glaciated mountains to the west and south. My Wyoming was not stunningly beautiful in the conventional sense, but had a rare honest rawness all its own. Driving toward the glaciated mountains now, west against the wind, we pass through an area where strange shafts of rock once stood on a sandstone ledge. Some of the shafts were said to be ten feet high. Back in the 1930s the Wyoming Writers' Project reported on these odd monuments said to be created by sheepherders who longed for company. Some of the shafts resembled human profiles.

Nasim and I drove out here one afternoon when I was fifteen, trying to find those shafts of carved rock. We took the back roads. It was January and the weather was mild; most of the previous week's snowfall had melted or blown away. Where the road lay straight for miles, she let me drive. The old 1963 Falcon, one of two cars her husband had meticulously maintained for years, had a stick shift. I was okay driving it once I reached cruising speed in third gear.

However, having to use second and first gears caused me great anxiety.

"Turn there," she suddenly said and pointed. I wasn't about to downshift to second. Instead of braking I just turned the steering wheel. We careened onto a dirt road in a spray of gravel, nearly sliding into a ditch. I swerved back onto the washboard and we bounced along in third gear for five rattling miles while Nasim stared hard out the window.

"Okay," she said finally. "It's just over that rise. Robert and I saw them years ago on a picnic."

I topped the hill and pressed the brake down, remembering at the last moment to punch in the clutch with my other foot. We stopped. I sighed. So far, so good. I hadn't killed the engine or hit anything. Nasim raised her binoculars, scanning the bare land. Even without binoculars I could see there were no stone shafts. Just more sagebrush.

"They have to be here. I know it was this road." She scowled and smacked her fist against the dashboard. I said nothing.

"Turn the car around," she barked. "I know they're here somewhere."

I told her I didn't know how. She laughed suddenly, then talked me through it. Following her orders, I shifted into reverse, gave it a little gas, gently raised my foot from the clutch, then shifted—gave it—gently raised—and so on, until we were pointed south again. I drove the five miles back out onto the highway, then we sped west a few more miles and repeated the whole scenario at the next county road. Each time the dashboard suffered under her clenched fist, but at least I was honing my skills in turning the car around without killing the engine. The clutch, however, was probably in a sorry state.

At last Nasim leaned her head against the window and dropped the binoculars in her lap. "Let's go home," she said in a small voice.

As we headed back toward Laramie, she still appeared dejected at not being able to find the stone shafts. "Maybe people knocked them down," I said. "Maybe the wind tipped them over and they broke."

"The wind goes through the stone, not around it," she said.

"Through?"

"Did I say that? Don't ask me why I said that. I don't know what's wrong with me. I wanted so much to show them to you. They were so eerie and lonely. They reminded me of those heads on Easter Island, even though they were supposed to be of gods. These stones were meant to remind the carver of certain people. Can you imagine being so lonely that you would go to all the trouble of carving a person out of a solid piece of sandstone?"

I couldn't imagine. Family, friends, school, books, my dog, flute lessons, all crowded my life. Certainly I had experienced loneliness. And not necessarily when I was alone. I wondered, had Nasim been that lonely?

When we reached Brees Field, Laramie's tiny airport west of town—just a hangar, a little terminal, and some broad runways—she suddenly remembered that I had only a learner's permit, and she made me stop to switch places with her.

"If we rented an airplane, we could look for the stones," I suggested.

"I refuse to fly," she said. "Every time I get on a plane I have to prepare to meet my Maker. It gets tiring always getting ready to die, so now I don't fly."

"I like to fly," I boasted. "Our family flies to all sorts of places."

We had reached my neighborhood. "Which street is yours?" she asked as the streetlights began to switch on, one by one, in the gathering darkness.

"Duna. That one." How could she forget? She'd been to our house before.

"Of course, there it is. What does Duna mean?" she asked me.

"I don't know." I opened the car door.

"You don't know?" She looked at me disapprovingly and some of her usual peppery vigor seemed to return.

"I think it's Spanish."

"You think? You should know," she retorted. "You should know the significance of the name of your street. You should know where the prevailing winds blow from when they hit your house. You should know where your drinking water comes from, what geological formation your house sits on, what indigenous species once lived where your yard lies and what tribes hunted here. If you don't know that, then you are just another damned urban nomad whose feet have temporarily stopped moving."

"I know some of that," I protested.

"Do you? What are ten wildflowers that bloom in the Laramie Basin?"

"Goodbye," I said. "I'm late for dinner."

In my own way I thought I did know. I just wasn't interested in dissecting my prairie and separating out its parts. I saw the whole picture, the sum of the parts, and loved and knew it intuitively. Later, I figured Nasim wanted me to open my squeezed-shut eyes and actually see what I'd been touching and stumbling over in my blind love of the prairie, because an open-eyed love is deeper than a blind love. She didn't want me to be someone who loved blindly.

We never did find those shafts of stone, nor the sandstone ledge on which they supposedly stood, although we went out looking one more time. Maybe in the melting and freezing episodes of a Wyoming winter the ground heaved and toppled them. Or maybe cattle looking for a nibble or a back scratch tipped them over. Perhaps since it was over half a century since she'd seen them, searching was pointless. Maybe she had forgotten where they were. Perhaps someday I will stumble upon them some early June day, as I tramp across the prairie, muddy and windblown, looking for something else. Then the surprise will be as great as the delight of discovery, even if the shafts of stone are toppled and in pieces.

❧ ❧ ❧

We are an hour out of town now, driving west through southern Wyoming at a speed that would have seemed as fast as light a hundred years ago. We travel in minutes the distance it took pioneers a day to cover. For many people, a drive across southern Wyoming is best accomplished at a speed approaching that of light, with as little interaction with the landscape as possible from a case of glass and steel on a combustion engine. But I'm not driving. I'm navigating.

As navigator, I feel obliged to look out the window, witness the land as it scrolls by, and take any gifts it may have to offer the eyes.

Instantly I see thin, twin cuttings of tire tracks in the snow on the side of a small hill. Maybe a rancher's truck brought hay to an isolated herd this morning. Amid the tracks, a reddish-brown creature trots in the snow. I press my face against the glass. Too small for deer or antelope, it's a coyote. A gift. "Look!" I cry. A second later, we've driven several hundred feet past it. Only then do heads turn. Too late. I try to return the gift by leaving a track of words on a snowy page, here….

Driving on, we scroll across the landscape into afternoon. And Utah. A sign tells us so. We coast down a narrow canyon, suspended in fog. Curving down the six-percent grade in the fog, it seems we are caught on an endless downward spiral into nothingness. To those who dislike enclosed spaces, a canyon is bad enough. But a canyon wrapped in fog is a white hell—especially since I am now driving. I grip the steering wheel with sweaty hands and remind myself to keep breathing.

At last the road seems to level. Buildings appear as gray shadows, then disappear back into the fog. We drive along a great dike. Suddenly the road crowns the dike and we are looking out from the edge of a precipice. It's the Great Salt Lake, which today mimics the color of fog, which mimics sky, which mimics the pewter gray mud at the lake's edge. One can't tell where lake ends and sky begins, which is mud and which is water. Where a spit of land juts out, it seems to hang over the edge of the world.

We cross miles of salt flats. I had expected them to be white and dry as bone dust, but they too are gray as the fog. Piles of round stones scattered across the sheets of mud break the gray into patterns of charcoal and silver. Where did these rocks come from? Did the lake cough them up? Were they the skipping stones of giants?

"You can read them," my son Ben mutters as he stares out the window. "The stones. They spell words."

We all stare from the car. Suddenly the random scatterings and patterns of dark and light become large letters. Fields of letters flow by: initials of lovers, connected by huge plus signs; names of football teams, of basketball teams. Connect the dots and stones become thoughts.

It's graffiti of sorts. But while spray-painted slogans and carved initials disgust me, this form astounds me. Here is evidence not just of human arrogance, but of the immense silliness of our species. Imagine the work it took to pick up truckloads of stones in the mountains or riverbeds to haul out to these flats, then to arrange them perfectly so as to form twenty, thirty, forty-foot long letters and words, only to spell such banal sentiments as GO UTES, JAZZ #1, WS + TR. Imagine the work it took. That's what we say about Stonehenge and Carnac and Easter Island. But there we assume a greater significance than the bald confession of an individual's love for a team.

The wind skates past us toward Wyoming as we slip into Nevada, into sudden calm. Extreme landscapes of light and rock form Nevada. My idea of beauty suddenly stretches wider to encompass these raw peaks. In my valley back home, the wind seems to have sanded the sharp edges off the mountains, but here, these jagged burnt umber and copper-streaked mountains seem newly formed, untouched by wind or water.

Christmas dinner in Elko. Where else but in a casino? Hot lights bounce off cool slabs of mirrors and every surface is either light or reflected light. Cameras watch our smallest gestures; we huddle in a group in the middle of the dining tables, self-consciously a family among singles and couples. While we eat, a basketball game on a big-screen television blares the only human voices we hear, other than our own, as the rest of the people around us, plump, pink-skinned men and women in their fifties and sixties, methodically shovel chicken-fried steak into their mouths, hurrying to get back to the slot machines. Disoriented, I realize that this artificial environment could be anywhere in the world, Florida or Europe or a cruise ship in the Caribbean. But later, in the windy darkness of the parking lot, a sense of place returns. We are not just anywhere. We stand on the western side of the North American continent, in desert country, headed for the ocean.

The next day, the invisible pull of the tides drags us through the Sierra Nevadas and down the long incline to the flat land around Sacramento. By day's end we are threading a labyrinth of highways and exits to cross Altamont Pass, then circle the light-studded waters of San Francisco Bay, and finally arrive at our destination, a lovely new hotel plunked down amidst a deserted office park.

Morning seeps in through a paste of gray clouds, revealing pieces here and there of a gray, foggy valley. My sister's wedding is on the 28th, which leaves us this one day to explore northern California. Used to sunshine and mountains as compass points, we lose all sense of direction and must follow my sister and her fiancé, who insist the ocean is "this way" and not the direction I think we should be going. Paper map and mental map do not agree until we stand on the shore.

Living in a land-locked region has made me forget how powerful the ocean is. I can't stop staring at the stormy waves and dashing spray. My children stand slightly behind me, using me as a shield. They have never seen the ocean before. Tall waves gray as sheet metal lunge toward us, as we huddle together at the edge of the continent, and it seems we will be engulfed. Then the waves crumple and crash at our feet, and a blast of salty wind sands our cheeks. My children turn their backs to the Pacific.

I don't understand them; we don't share the same thoughts after all. I could never turn my back on these heaving waves. Long after the family has gone back to the car, I stay by the water, feeling like I'm the only person on the planet. I realize I'm keeping watch, as if the waves will stop their regular thumping if I so much as look away. But now I know how the wind would look if we could see it. It would take the form of these wild, seven-foot waves buckling against the sand. For the moment I'm glad that the wind, at least, is invisible. Then I realize that the wind that touches my cheek in Wyoming comes partly from this ocean and its waves. The Pacific's gales drive the woolly blizzards across Wyoming. The winds that dance across these waves will in days to come fuel the local winds that shred the snow and scorch the skin of grass in the Laramie Basin to a scoured gold.

As I stand on the beach, a sentinel, rain whips my face like the knife-edges of cordgrass. I hear a roar. Is it ocean or wind or both? Or something even greater? I remember the squall winds whose names Nasim taught me: *chocolatero, chubasco, williwaw.* One blows off the Gulf of Mexico, one off the Pacific coast of Mexico, one off the coast of Alaska. To name the winds is to acknowledge them, their place in our lives, and our role as witness to their power. Unfortunately, on this day I can think of no better name for this one than *damn wind.*

Leaving the edge of the world, I scurry inland to the car, past a deserted amusement park as the wind whistles around the base of the peeling wooden roller coaster, making the structure sway. Some days are better left for the wind's amusement alone.

On our last morning in California the sun comes out and mountains and landmarks suddenly appear. Like prisoners let out of a padded isolation cell, we relish the sunshine, the clear hard-edged view of mountains to the south, and the thin disc of blue bay edging San Francisco to the north. Eastward lies our road and now we cross in daylight what we'd traversed in darkness. Grass-covered hills rise like smooth brontosaurus backs from the valley floor. Something about these hills captivates me: they are massive and yet comfortingly round, with a hide of thick, yellow grass and no trees or structures to ruin their cartoonish shape. They look as though they were drawn by a child with a big wheat-colored crayon. I want to draw them myself, or photograph them; I want to run my hands over them and feel the rough, hairy grass curve beneath me. Bare but not barren, gentle to the eye, these hills call to me. We must stop!

Instead, we drive on, carried along on a current of rush-hour traffic. As the morning traffic thins, we drive across Altamont Pass, east of San Francisco, and suddenly enter a strange wonderland. Thousands of tall silver towers have been planted on the sides of the bare hills like a strange metallic forest. On each tower, blades spin in the wind. They are wind turbines, descendants of the lowly windmill, generating electricity for California power companies. We drive by, open-mouthed. Then the question we all are thinking is voiced by my husband: "Why aren't there some of these near Laramie?"

∾ ∾ ∾

Eight years later, our question is answered: we get a chance to tour a new wind farm not far from Laramie, guests of the company, SeaWest, that runs it. Early on a Saturday morning Curt and I, his siblings and their families, his parents, and our sons, pile into five vehicles and drive a half hour westward across the Laramie Basin. Even from miles away, the wind farm stands out, silvery white rods perched on a ridge, seemingly tiny and delicate. Exiting Interstate 80 at Arlington, population twenty or so, perspective changes as we draw nearer, and we realize the spires are actually tall towers. On the bluff above the local gas station run three rows of one hundred white towers. Each row extends for several miles, towers gleaming in the morning sun. On the top of each 180-foot tall tower spin three long white blades—propellers—facing into the wind like giant pinwheels. These graceful white creations are the highest high-tech answer to the windmill. And the most elegant.

My husband's father John, a professor of atmospheric science at the University of Wyoming, helped research and select the site for these wind turbine towers on the Foote Creek rim near Arlington. It's the site of some of the strongest and most constant winds in the western United States. Now that he is retiring from the university, as a special treat, we get a tour of the site.

We divide our group, climb into two four-wheel drive vehicles and bump along a dirt trail that parallels the west side of Interstate 80, then we duck under the interstate through a truck-sized culvert and head eastward across the rising prairie. In our vehicle, driven by a businessman who helped to finance the wind farm, we have crammed my husband and me, his sister, two of his brothers, and two of our sons. As we snake up the north side of the ridge to the top of the rim, Curt and his siblings pepper our driver with questions. How much did each turbine cost? How fast do the blades spin? Where does the power go? What is the effect on the environment?

As the magical-looking white towers loom closer, our driver matches each question with an answer: one million dollars each; over two hundred miles an hour at the blade tips; into the Pacific Northwest power grid; virtually nil, though there was unfounded concern about the safety of curious hawks.

Finally, as we reach the top, the questions stop and we step out into a river of rushing wind that hinders more talk. We stand on top of the bluff, on top of the world. Eight thousand feet above sea level, with limitless blue sky stretching above us, we scan mile after mile of patchwork terrain: meadows down to the south of the bluff, prairie to the west, rolling hills to the north and west. To the east, a long low line of faded blue marks the humped back of the Laramie Mountains. To the south, distant peaks mark Colorado. Below our feet, at the base of the bluff, lies the greasy gas station and beyond it the tiny twin lines of the interstate. Above the rumbling of the wind in my ears, I can hear the whine of the nearest turbine and the faint *whoosh, whoosh,* of the giant blades spinning. One of the little boys in the family runs toward the nearest tower but several of us stop him. I don't know if there is any danger, as the blades don't reach more than halfway down the tower's span, but still the way they slice through the air makes one nervous about allowing a child to stand underneath. Three of the little boys pose together a couple hundred feet from the tower. They face into the wind, which slicks their hair back and plasters their sweaters against their chests. They look even smaller than they really are on this great stretch of prairie ridge, beneath these tall towers.

To the north of the ridge, hawks float, riding the rising thermal currents. In older wind turbine designs the open tower structures made ideal nesting places for birds. Unfortunately, they often got caught in the blades when leaving or arriving at their nests. These Wyoming towers were designed as enclosed columns to prevent hawks and other birds from nesting at all. Additionally, each row of these towers was set back from the edge of the rim so as not to interrupt the rising flight patterns of the hawks. Too, the rows had to be carefully placed with respect to the other rows of wind turbines. Too close and the downwind turbines wouldn't spin to their potential. Too far away and there wouldn't be enough room on the ridge for all the towers.

A man walks along the road beneath the towers, coming toward us. He carries a tripod and camera and looks ragged from the wind's touch. He says he climbed the bluff, straight up from the gas station below, to take some photographs of the wind turbines. Technically, he's trespassing. The businessman speaks to him, then he heads back down the bluff. At least he got some photographs, probably pretty good ones considering how close he was to the towers.

My youngest son Alex and I hunker down on the golden prairie grass beside one of the vehicles, attempting to find some shelter from the wind. It does seem that lower down to the ground, at the level of grasses, the wind batters one less. Or maybe not.

I wonder how this day will be imprinted on his mind. Will he remember the force of this wind as it slams across the rim? The fragile beauty of the silvery blades seen spinning from a distance? The family standing together on the windy ridge watching the blades turn? And what exactly do I wish he would remember—the power of nature or the accidental beauty of human-made things? Or both? Certainly, the awe we feel at the immensity of forces at work here—both the intense wind and the technology of the blades' weight, speed, and grace in dancing with nature—is greater than any man-made dam or skyscraper we've ever seen. After all, if the artist Christo could stretch an orange curtain across a gap between two bluffs in Colorado's wilderness and call it art, aren't these giant pinwheels, looking deceptively simple, a kind of sculpture too, though anointed with meaning and function by businessmen and scientists, not artists? Is there any harm in these wind turbines being here? Would not Nasim celebrate the human imagination, effort, ingenuity, care, and knowledge that created and situated these towering wind-blown blades?

At the least I hope Alex remembers his grandfather had a hand in it. But I don't think that he will want to remember this wind or this great, scoured prairie. He's too cold and tired.

∾ ∾ ∾

"We are acquainted with a mere pellicle of the globe on which we live," Thoreau wrote. "Most have not delved six feet beneath the surface, nor leaped as many above it. We know not where we are." Nasim would have agreed. She tried to tell me so, but I didn't listen well.

The wind meanders past the walls of the house like a trout swimming down a lazy stream; it nuzzles some willow bushes, then shimmies out onto the prairie. Snow that fell in the night scatters in white whirlwinds in its wake. I stand at the door and watch the wind work.

The wind knows the curve of the land, the pressure of the atmosphere, the texture of cumulus and cirrus and altostratus. It is intimate with the entire planet. I once knew a patch of land that is now altered beyond recognition. But at least I know which way is north and where the edge of the continent is. I know where I am: home.

And I know you, wind. You rode landward across the waves. When the ocean retreated, you kept going. You swept seven cities in one blow and called yourself mighty. You made the evening news. You played and tossed in the grasses on the hills above Milpitas. You skipped across the Great Salt Lake. You turned the blades of a hundred insignificant pinwheels

at Arlington, Wyoming. I am not afraid of you. Go
ahead, let me see you. Topple some stones. Blow
through my clothes. Let me hear you roar.

CHINOOK WIND

Deep winter

STILL WATER IN a side pool of the Laramie River floats a looking-glass world of cirrus clouds and sky. Nothing moves. The wind is still and all else holds its breath. A glance around becomes a checklist of assurances that the wind has quit blowing: the chokecherry bushes don't sway; the cottonwood's remaining brown leaves don't flutter down; the musty tiles of dry leaves in the ground's hollows seem laid down as securely as linoleum. But it's only temporary. Soon the twigs will quiver; soon the fallen leaves will lift an edge, flip, skitter across the hard dirt; the chokecherry branches will bob as if pulled by invisible threads. After all, the wind must blow, the planet must breathe.

Two days ago, the chinook winds screamed across the plains like runaway horses. In some rooms of this house, the shriek of wind never stopped; though the windows were tightly shut, they vibrated with every blast as though made of cellophane. Wave after wave shook the walls. Joists creaked. Dirt and dead leaves sprayed the windows.

On the highway the wind picked up a truck and flipped it over. Police officers directing traffic around the wreck could hardly stand up under the force of the gale. Backs to it, they leaned against it as if about to sit down. One of the officers turned sideways to motion to a car and the wind stretched his face oddly at the cheeks. His hair stood out from his head as if he'd been electrocuted.

At night, the roar of the wind against the windows sounded like surf washing against the shore. I realized I hadn't seen any birds in two days, neither sparrow nor starling nor chickadee. Either they were clinging with a rigor-mortis-like grip to some half-sheltered fir branch or had been blown to Cheyenne or Scottsbluff and would have to wing it home later in the week.

If George had been around, he would have been blowing across the land with the birds. George was a Border collie whom Nasim said was part dog and part wind. Her husband Robert had grown up on a ranch north of Laramie and had always kept a

Border collie, even after he moved to town, became an accountant, and married Nasim. But unlike the others he'd owned, this dog had no sense. George was odd: he seemed to think the wind was a living thing. Let out of the yard for even a moment, he'd chase the wind right out of town and across the prairie. And when the big winds came in deep winter, he'd really go berserk. One February he sprinted six miles south to the cement plant, across railroad tracks, busy streets, and stockyards, chasing a north wind south. Another February he ran almost to the mouth of Telephone Canyon, where a trucker stopped and grabbed him before he could cause an accident on the highway.

But finally one day—again in February— George ran so hard he caught the wind. Some women feeding their horses up near the Sherman Hill subdivision east of Laramie saw a white-and-black blur cross the prairie with the wind at its back. As it shot past them, they realized it was a dog. Then they marveled that his fur was streaming out behind him. He'd outrun the wind, which should have been blowing his fur the other way. Then suddenly the dog rolled in the dirt, kicking up a cloud of dust. They ran over to look: the dog was dead. At first they thought someone had shot him, but the vet said later that George had had massive heart failure. George was the last Border collie

Robert kept. He and Nasim hung his collar and tags out under the eaves, as a wind chime of sorts, and buried George's body beneath one of the three cottonwood trees by their stone house.

Now in the calm morning air I open the door and see a red line of dust sprinkled across the threshold. A magic line. A marker. The wind's own boundary, beyond which it could not carry more than the finest dust motes. Those motes spill from the curtains as I open the blinds. In the linen closet, a faint red veil of dust rises from the towels when they are shaken. A thin layer of red powders my skin, too. The chinook wind has left its signature.

The chinook descends the lee slope of a mountain, having left all its moisture on the windward side, and becomes a dry, thirsty wind that eats through drifts of snow in no time. It sucks the moisture out of earth and trees, sandblasts windshields with a fine grit, snaps branches and shatters windows. It floods the valleys with rivers of roaring air. Chinook has brothers and sisters around the world: *papagayos* in Costa Rica; *reshabar* out of the high Caucasus Mountains in Asia; *yumo oroshi* in Japan; Santa Ana in California. All are dry, hot, downward-blowing winds.

For two days we have been surrounded by this battering chinook wind and I've noticed my family begin to get nervous, snapping at each other like mean old turtles. The wind is a living thing, angry and fierce, and it's easy to feel that we have been living under siege. But now not only the morning is still, but afternoon as well. We come out of our house, assess damage, then rest. We have earned it.

I used to ride a horse named Hazel along the willow bottomlands at the foot of the Snowy Range near Centennial. She was a tall, young buckskin mare, sleek and lively, a tawny dun color with a black mane and tail. Seemingly docile and well-broke, Hazel, I soon realized, suffered riders only so long. When she'd had enough, the roller coaster ride began. The reins, the bit, the wide Western saddle were all mere props as far as she was concerned. My nonchalant air of competency faded fast as I'd cling to the saddle horn wondering whether this time I'd be thrown off or merely swiped like a large white rag against the nearest corral fence. I was supposed to show her who was master, but she knew, as did I, that it wasn't me.

Think of nature as a horse named Hazel. For many of us in urban places, nature is a docile thing, seen at a picnic area in the mountains, a corner of a city park, an open field between housing developments, a well-traveled highway in a national park.

Lulled into underestimating the natural world, we view nature as toothless and innocent, a decorative thing, as pretty and non-threatening as the colorful photographs of wildflowers and mountain lakes in Sierra Club calendars. But let one small mishap occur—one's car breaks down on a lonely desert road between cities, or one gets trapped on the open plains during a sudden blizzard, or one gets lost on a seemingly simple shortcut on a mountain trail—and nature becomes in-your-face rude and unruly, bucking its rider off its slippery back.

While driving at night from Laramie to Casper, two and a half hours north, I often feel a gnawing uneasiness. The shorter way to Casper is to cut north through Shirley Basin, instead of taking Interstate 25, which swings in a more leisurely curve from Cheyenne. I take the shortcut, but pay for it in terms of loneliness. When the road descends into Shirley Basin, suddenly the familiar radio stations fuzz into static. Two or three dots of light mark far outposts on the other side of the basin a ranch or two, perhaps. When I was a kid, Kerr-McGee ran a large uranium mine operation in Shirley Basin. Employees of the mine carpooled from Casper to work every day, leaving the mine at night for the odd coyote or antelope to roam. The mine was shut down in the 1980s and the workers left. The coyotes and the antelope remained, however, along with a few buildings where the mine offices were. These days, if a car should happen to break down here in Shirley Basin, help would be a long time coming.

But driving through Shirley Basin at night never seemed to bother Nasim. She could drive as slowly as she wanted, trundling along at thirty miles an hour to gaze at the Little Dipper and Orion's Belt hanging so low and bright in the bowl of the sky, or she could mash the accelerator to the floor and blast past the ninety-mile mark on her speedometer; she could drive down the wrong side of the road for forty miles or even drive with her clothes off. But she kept the radio on, even when it was just static, as a reminder of the human world far removed from this dark lonely one.

Me, I drive as fast as I can across Shirley Basin, hopeful that I won't hit the jackrabbits and prairie dogs that scurry across just in front of my path, thankful for the thin warm shell of metal, glass, and upholstery that hurtles me down the road.

Fear is not so bad, Nasim told me once. I was the kind of kid who always found something to dread, whether it was being called upon in class, not finding a seat on the school bus, hearing my enemies giggling at me behind my back, or merely wearing a different brand of jeans than the other girls. Nasim tried to cure me of these fears by reminding me of the big ones— the fear that shake the foolishness out of your head and make you suddenly think clearly, the kinds of fear where more is at stake than who said what and who likes whom.

To illustrate her point, she told me about her winter camping adventure as a teenager when she'd run away with a young man to a deep snowy valley in the Neversummer Range. Now, at least fifty years later, her cheeks turned pink as she answered my question—yes, he was her boyfriend. They had told no one where they were going, and maybe they wouldn't come back. Maybe they would live off the land, build a house deep in the wilderness, hunt and fish and gather berries and nuts for their food. Planning and scheming, they packed up his car and drove up into the mountains one winter's morning when they should have been in their high school homerooms.

Wickedly cold winds sliced at their packs as they got out of the car at their destination, but they didn't care. Hand in hand, they walked in brilliant sunlight to the mouth of a valley beneath jagged peaks. Miles from anyone, they stopped beside a snow-covered creek beneath a grove of Douglas fir and set their packs down. He had brought a tent and she had stolen her brother's Boy Scout sleeping bags, some cans of food, and a tiny, cranky gas stove that refused to get hotter than lukewarm.

As the sun slid behind the peaks, they tramped the snow down and set up the tent, then went separate ways to look for firewood. In daylight, confidence had overflowed in her heart, and she had laughed and chattered gaily with the boy. But as the light faded, the back of her neck tingled and she felt like a rabbit about to be snatched up by a hawk. Knee-deep in snow, she was bent over hunting for wood when she sensed the precise moment night fell: the forest around her turned black and the snow turned a pale, luminous blue.

Her hands and the wood were shadowed. The sky was suddenly dark too, with no stars out at all. She looked for the way back to camp but couldn't remember which way she'd come. A thin worm of panic burrowed into her gut as she hugged her bundle of wood and scanned the shadows. Her voice was gone. She couldn't call out to her companion. The worm of panic grew larger inside her. She couldn't breathe. She couldn't see. But suddenly her legs began to move and she stumbled toward her right, catching her coat on branches, sinking thigh-deep in snow, but clutching her wood and wading onward.

Then she saw her friend crouched over a wick-thin flame, feeding it bits of dry pine. She crashed through the forest to his side and dropped her load of wood by the tent. He didn't even look up. She didn't tell him of feeling lost, of the panic that had nearly swallowed her up; instead she watched him as he tenderly nursed the flame. Under his almost motherly attention, the flame twisted higher like a pale shoot of some rare plant. Feeling as small and thin as that flame, Nasim watched, afraid to say a word, afraid almost to breathe for fear of blowing the fire out.

At last the flame latched onto a big dry pine chip and took root. Her companion relaxed and Nasim began to breathe again. Carefully she knelt beside him and they sheltered the fire with their bodies, feeding it more bits of wood until it grew large. Then they sat back and basked in its soothing warmth.

"I thought of us as flames too, in a way," Nasim told me. "We are lit and left to burn, and the winds and cold and darkness do their best to blow us out, but somehow we keep burning. That's all you can do sometimes, just stay lit long enough to shed some light and give a little warmth."

That night, they clung together in their sleeping bags as the winds blew down off the peaks and shook their tent. She couldn't sleep. She wondered if maybe the sun would not rise the next morning, for the first time in millions of years, and the world would remain in darkness. "I think this is how prehistoric people used to feel on a long winter's night," she said. "That's why they invented stories and songs to keep their minds busy and gods to keep them company."

When the sun walked their way at dawn, Nasim was ready to cry for joy. It seemed like a miracle that the sun had risen, after the dark pit of the night before. By the time her companion woke up, Nasim had packed everything but the tent and his sleeping bag and was ready to hike back out to the car. "My one attempt at living a wild and beautiful life," she said. That was it for her—no more camping, no living off the land, no running away with handsome young men. She graduated from high school, got a job as a secretary in a law office in Laramie, and married the young accountant whose office was next door. Nature was relegated to Nasim's backyard for the next fifty-odd years.

ᔓ ᔓ ᔓ

Young children don't question whether nature should be or can be controlled or used. Rocks and sand and trees are to be explored and water is to be splashed in or dammed. As a child, I couldn't sit for long by a stream without jumping up to alter its flow with rocks and logs. When I was older, I spent one summer trying to transplant wildflowers from the prairie into my garden. None of them took to the artificially rich soil and steady diet of water, and in August I had a patch of bare dirt and dried stems.

Among the boys I grew up with, gopher hunting with pellet gun or sharpened stick was considered a form of recreation. Target shooting, using live prairie dogs for targets, was not unheard of either. And many of my classmates, boys and girls alike, hunted antelope and elk in the fall. We were given two days off from school each autumn during hunting season so students could go hunting up on Elk Mountain or down in Shirley Basin.

But this is penny-ante stuff. Humans can pull so many strings to balance and unbalance nature that it would seem we are nearly godlike in our power. But instead of being competent gods, we are like incompetent puppet masters. When we pull a string, more often than not the effect is that of a noose for some species or ecosystem.

Consider the example of a Colorado town with the best of intentions. In a city-owned field grows a species of rare wild orchid. The city "resource managers" wanted to encourage its growth and found that the orchid thrives if the field where it takes root is mowed at a particular stage in the orchid growth cycle.

But when the mowing machines came to the field at the proper time, the workers found that this stage occurs when the field's other residents, the bobolinks, are nesting and raising their young.

What is a good resource manager to do? Establish a hierarchy of value. Orchids are rarer than bobolinks in this area, hence more "valuable." But baby bobolinks shredded by city mowing machines make for bad publicity. Okay, so find another solution. Move the bobolink nests to another field and establish that field as "managed" for bobolinks and the first field as "managed" for wild orchids. Try to justify that to the county commissioners in next year's budget or to the birders on their monthly birdwalk. Poor humans. No matter what our intentions, when we interfere we cause harm.

Above the front doors of the University of Wyoming's engineering building where Curt and I studied drafting, a motto is chiseled in the sandstone lintel: "The control of nature is won, not given." Walking across Prexy's Pasture on the way to class, half-blinded by blowing dust or half-eaten by frenzied mosquitoes, I doubted that nature could ever be controlled. But if it could, I agreed that such control would have to be wrested in a bloody battle, not handed over gift-wrapped with a card.

Nasim was a good influence on me—a tree-hugger with common sense, not the "humans-are-bad-and-don't-belong-on-this-planet" kind of environmentalist. Nor was she the opposite type who believes that all of nature was put here by God strictly for human use, Planet Earth as blank check. We must eat and live, but do as little harm as possible, she would say. Nasim taught me a prayer the Maya offered before clearing a cornfield. She used it when she began her spring gardening, and she had taught it to her husband to say before he went hunting. Robert was a good man and didn't laugh at her, but his eyes would twinkle as he kissed her goodbye before leaving on a hunting trip. "Now how does that prayer go?" he would ask, knowing full well how it went. It went like this:

Now I make you an offering, that you may be warned:
I am about to molest your heart.
I am going to dirty you, I am going to work you
In order that I may live.

Such a prayer wouldn't hurt any rider on the ornery horse called Nature. It might even help ease the pain when, once again, we are bucked off.

FEATHER MERCHANT WIND

~ ~ ~ ~ ~ ~

False spring

~ SPRING CREEK IS running golden. Along its banks, the willows are turning from grayish brown to yellow. It reminds me of the childhood experiment: a white carnation is placed in a glass of red-colored water. As the carnation stem imbibes the water, the flower turns pink. As the willow roots steep in the golden creek, their branches become golden rods. It's more of a poetic notion than scientific fact, of course, but appealing nonetheless.

Knowing the willows, it's not Spring Creek but spring that is changing them. Or at least the promise of spring to come. The cottonwoods, too, have been taken in by this false spring—their branches look less gray and more yellow; their buds swell with coiled leaves waiting inside, ready to unwind

143

their soft green tissues at the slightest hint of warmth. The trees have been fooled by this warm weather into thinking it's the end of April, but that's six weeks from now. If I could, I would warn them of the snows that will come before then. But they run on their own clocks and tree history is older than my history. There is nothing for it but to trust the process of growth.

"Who am I to fuss over them?" Nasim asked, half laughing, half scornful, when I pointed out crocuses and tulips blooming too early. "Find something else to worry about, please."

Still, even now, I remark on the thickening buds and yellowing branches to anyone who will listen, as if our united concern will make a difference. The wind has been nasty these past days, kicking up dust and bending young trees—a much more interesting topic of conversation. With it travels a cold front, flapping its snowy wings. At dusk Curt, the children, and I are leaving Laramie yet again, driving south across the valley floor. Wine-dark clouds shutter most of the sky, except for a round opening to the west, which reveals a ragged circle of lighter-colored sky. New snowflakes drift across the road, which is as slick as a newly varnished hardwood floor. We leave soft white sawdust in our wake. Pale and quiet, the boys voluntarily buckle their seatbelts; infant Alex is already asleep. Our timing, as usual, is bad: it seems we're always coming or going in storms, though we don't plan it that way. The circle of lighter sky is a circle of hope, I decide, as I watch it while crossing the valley. Perhaps it's a circle of hope for some pilot tonight flying into Brees Field: no need to navigate through clouds as rough as cement mixers, just fly in straight as a needle through fabric. Maybe our journey, too, will be needle-straight simple, once we get to the shelter of the mountains further south.

As we climb the hill to the summit, the sky clears and I tip my head against the cold window to stare at the stars. My husband tells me about riding on this stretch of highway as a kid, when his family would make their monthly trip down to Colorado to stock up on groceries at the less expensive market in Fort Collins. The Cadillac his family drove back then, a finned monstrosity from the early sixties, was equipped with an important feature—a back window ledge broad enough for a kid to stretch out on full length. Curt would lie there as his father drove the family home to Laramie, the darkness rushing past just on the other side of the glass, the stars within arm's reach.

Now he is the one driving as the tiny blue-white light of a satellite glides by hundreds of miles above us. Jupiter glows steadily and the three bright stars of Orion's belt seem to float in a dark pool. Feeling rather small and trying not to think about how the stars will be shining long after I am gone, I decide to label the middle star as my soul's final resting place, should the Pearly Gates not be an option. If I must leave this messy, wonderful planet sooner rather than later, as this dark, forbidding landscape warns, then let me believe I'll just travel to a distant star and dangle from one of its cartoon points with a pair of binoculars in my hand for watching the action on Earth.

As if reading my mind's lonely thoughts, my husband snaps on the radio and tunes it to a basketball game. Surrounded by the stereo voices of cheering crowds and excited announcers, we drive on. But as we round a curve we see in the distance an ominous cluster of headlights and flashing red lights. Soon we see why: a wrecker is hooking up to a mangled van, and nearby stretch two jackknifed semis. Police with clipboards and tape measures confer, but luckily the ambulances are long gone. The children look on silently as we are guided past long black skid marks and pieces of crumpled metal. The wind, at least, is not to blame for this. Ice and darkness, two eternal enemies of humans, and a new one, speed, are to blame.

We continue our descent into the sheltering hills near the state line and down to Virginia Dale.

The children close their eyes and use each other as pillows. I look up through the window and study Orion's belt. Those three stars, so close together and lined up so true, seem placed there by design. But why must I seek intent in the universe, even in the placement of stars? Why can't I just accept randomness? Because that's the human way, to look for connections. The ancient Greeks, the Phoenicians, the Arabs, the Polynesians, the Arapaho, the Kiowa, probably even the old Germanic and Baltic tribes of my ancestors, all linked the stars to make pictures in the sky, warming the cold and indifferent darkness with stories. They placed themselves in relation to the rest of the universe by the act of naming the constellations they saw.

The names of the three stars of Orion's belt are Alnitak, Alnilam, and Mintaka. Some cultures saw them as the three eyes of a monster or the mouth of a devil, or the line of a deer's tail, but the Greeks saw them as the huntsman's belt. I rename them after the three boys sleeping in the back seat.

Truck after truck thunders past us, making up for lost time. My husband is not a slow driver, preferring to push the envelope in any driving conditions. But these rigs scream by at eighty-five plus down these snowy, narrow roads, as we watch them, silently incredulous at their drivers' arrogance. Our car shivers in their wake. After the convoy has gone by, the stars come back into view. Rigel and Betelgeuse anchor the corners of the Orion constellation, the only one I can pick out right now.

But we have entered the forested lowlands, time to watch for deer eyes reflecting our headlights by the side of the road. Now and then I sneak a look up at the sky. The stars are our thin tie to earlier travelers who crossed dark waters and deserts under the watchful eyes of their gods. Who watches us? I don't know anymore. Satellites. Aliens. God. Deer eyes.

One thought offers comfort on a cold, dark night, which is that we are made of the same stuff as those stars high in the sky. Calcium and iron in our bodies originated from supernovas that exploded long before our solar system was formed. Perhaps it's not mere dreaminess that causes humans to gaze at stars, but a profound connection too deep for words.

∾ ∾ ∾

Safely home again. The first rain of the year falls a week later, early in the morning. Streamers of silver float across the valley, leaving drops like clear glass marbles on the chokecherry bushes. A pause like the silence between movements of a symphony, then more rain, faster. A shift in the wind and the rain becomes heavier, splatting noisily on the pavement. Suddenly, silence: white powder is falling, leaving faint prints on the sidewalk. Trees, sagebrush, grass, all disappear.

At this time last year I was pregnant; my third child was a week overdue. Tired of waiting, I asked the obstetrician what triggered labor and received a hypothesis for an answer: it may not be the mother's body that triggers labor, but hormones sent from the baby's brain that prompt the mother's contractions. Untactfully, she added that a mother carrying a baby with no brain in its skull couldn't begin labor, as no signal could be sent from the baby. Medically interesting, but not the ideal message for a pregnant woman past her due date.

A year later, looking at the snow falling on the cottonwoods, my little boy beside me, I hope the buds won't leaf out until it is warm enough for them to grow. Perhaps my tenderness toward leaf buds comes from caring for Alex. He was born a few days after the doctor's remark, emerging from dark waters into a cool windy spring. Already a year has circled around him and he is facing his second spring on this planet. He looks up at the trees outside the window and points. A shiny black crow sits on one of the uppermost branches looking down at us.

This part of town, where the oldest and largest trees grow, we called the tree area, trees being noteworthy in Laramie. East and south and north of this central location, newer neighborhoods look bare for decades because a tree needs at least twenty years here to grow to a respectable size. As a kid newly arrived in Wyoming, I didn't realize this. When I watched my parents plant a knee-high spruce and a skinny birch, I began planning the tree house I would build. By the time I realized I would never build a tree house, having grown faster than the trees, I had already fallen in love with the treeless prairie behind our house.

Ironically, trees were in part the reason for Laramie's founding—that is, the nearby availability of trees. When the Union Pacific railroad began cutting west across Wyoming in the 1860s, the plains were as bare as they are now. This was a problem, because to make the ties for the rails to rest on, the railroaders needed trees. They found their source in the Medicine Bow Mountains and the Laramie Range, where forests grew whose trees were suitable for making railroad ties. So the railroaders made a camp near where Laramie is today, along the Laramie River between the two mountain ranges. A treatment plant still soaks the railroad ties with pungent creosote down by the rail-yard south of downtown.

Varying with altitude and climate, the trees found in the area include pines such as ponderosa, limber, and lodgepole; firs and spruces named Douglas, subalpine, Engelmann, and blue; aspens and cottonwoods. Each grows within a certain range of altitude above sea level. Hikers who know the land and the trees native to it can use them as natural altimeters to gauge how high they've climbed. As one travels higher in the Medicine Bow Mountains, cottonwoods give way to Engelmann spruce and subalpine fir. Just below the treeline where forests stop growing and ground-hugging tundra plants begin, the spruce and fir shrink and twist, thanks to the extreme weather, and become krummholz or "crooked wood." Some grow branches on just one side of their trunk, showing the struggle to survive against icy blasts of wind and snow. Their wood is gnarled, their appearance old and shriveled.

Above treeline, the tundra displays a multicolored weave of moss campion, forget-me-nots, and alpine lilies, many hundreds of years old. Small and delicate-looking, they have adapted to the aridity, altitude, and short growing season by staying low, blooming discreetly, and conserving moisture. Some plants barely extend three inches above the ground, though they may have been growing for over a hundred years.

Above the tundra, on the quartzite peaks of the Snowy Range, part of the Medicine Bow Mountains, grows the lonely survivor: lichen. Lichen is an understated little organism that consists of an alga and a fungus living together in a symbiotic relationship, like a man and a woman who are opposite types but find they complement each other. Lichen provides surprising dashes of color against the rocks: circles of brilliant orange, streaks of gold, splashes of vivid lime green.

Down in the valley where I live grows the settlers' favorite tree: cottonwoods. Call a cottonwood by any name—Fremont, lanceleaf, narrowleaf, Rio Grande, plains—the tree was a sign to weary travelers that water was nearby. Indians knew to make tea from the bark and poultices from the leaves. Only later have we learned that the bark of cottonwoods, willows, and aspen contains a substance resembling salicylic acid, a chemical in aspirin. Cotton falls from the female tree every spring, hence its common name. Green nodules on the twigs split open to release strings of soft creamy down. In late spring, falling cotton mimics the last snowstorm of the year as it drifts gently from the tree.

Nasim's three giant female cottonwoods shed their cotton across the grass, sidewalk, and fence around her house each spring. One day I came by Nasim's house and saw her high on an extension ladder in the arms of Erin, the second of the three giant cottonwoods. White cotton stuck to her hair, her shirt, and her skin.

"What are you doing?" I called up.

"Looking around," she replied. I held onto the ladder as she slowly descended. "My neighbor was trimming the branches for me and left the ladder up while he took a break, so I thought I'd climb up and see what it was like to be Erin, and Anne, and Nina."

"Why do you call them by girls' names?" I asked.

She looked down as though rearranging her thoughts, then squinted at me, the sunlight shining on her lined skin. "I always wanted daughters," she said. "I would have welcomed sons. What I got were trees. So, what the hell. A little naming doesn't hurt a thing. Do you think it's strange?"

I shook my head. "No. It's not strange. I always wanted a tree house, but I never got one and probably never will."

"Never say 'never,'" she said. "Come on, climb up. It's your turn. I'll hold it steady."

I looked up. The end of the ladder was way up there, at least two stories high. "I'm too heavy," I said. "I'm bigger than you already. I'll shake the ladder too much and you won't be able to hold it."

Her neighbor walked back over from his break, his tool belt jingling, chain saw in hand.

"Billy, would you hold this ladder for us?" Nasim asked. "She wants to go up in the tree and have a look around."

"Sure, Mrs. Sands." The man held the ladder with two hairy arms and looked expectantly at me. I blushed.

"Go ahead," Nasim said. Gripping the ladder, I carefully climbed, step over step, holding my breath nearly the whole time. About five rungs from the top I stopped, patted the tree's thick gray bark, then, with sweaty hands, started back down.

"Look around you at least," Nasim called. I stopped and studied the nearest branch, then climbed back down. The great tree house lover was afraid of heights.

As Billy readied his tools and ropes and lightly scaled the ladder, we sat down on the stone steps of the back porch. "I've hired a plane and pilot this afternoon. We're going to go flying," Nasim said.

"Flying? I thought you didn't like flying."

"I don't. Call your mother."

An hour later, we were at Brees Field. Quiet and thin, the pilot looked like my seventh-grade math teacher. He helped Nasim in, told us where to sit, and left us alone while he checked his instruments and started the engine. It sounded like a large lawn mower and Nasim raised her voice to be heard.

"I'd like you to fly low over the town and then up around the Laramie Mountains," she called to the pilot. He nodded. In minutes the plane was cruising down the runway, then suddenly the ground dropped away like a trap door and the little Cessna, with us in it, was climbing high above the valley floor. I looked over at Nasim. She was clutching her seatbelt and staring with great dismay at her feet.

"What's wrong? Are you going to be sick?" I asked.

"No," she said. "It's just that I've put on two different shoes." I raised my eyebrows and she laughed.

Suddenly I gasped. We'd already flown out over the park near my school, and now we were over the university. The twelve-story dormitories, the highest buildings in town, were little boxes. Then we winged over the high school, then above the little valley where my friend kept her horse, just south of W Hill. Ten years later that area where her horse had galloped alone would be filled in with houses, roads, and a junior high school. We flew above the bluffs to my neighborhood and over my house. My brother Eric stood in the driveway beside his bike, a tiny figure looking up at us. Over the ugly new houses sprouting on the prairie. Then south along the Laramie Mountains. Crimped rivulets and puckered gullies, rippling hills. The land looked like the hide of some great broad-backed cow, now smooth, now scuffed and scarred. The plane was flying higher now to clear the mountains and now and then the turbulence of the air currents would shake it and make it dip or weave.

Above the slabbed mounds of granite at Vedauwoo, halfway between Laramie and Cheyenne, the pilot turned the plane westward again, toward home. Nasim was still clutching her seatbelt, though she looked over at me and cracked a smile. I was too enthralled by the landscape below to be scared.

The landing back at Brees Field was smooth, though the wind near the ground seemed about to flip the plane over. After the pilot had taxied back to the shelter of the hangar, Nasim sighed heavily and looked over at me. After she climbed out, she slowly dropped to one knee as if straightening her wrinkled pantyhose and patted the ground.

After a moment, she got up, brushed off her hands and said briskly, "Well? What did you think?"

I said something about feeling very small and light up there. I thought, but didn't say, that I felt as tiny as a sparrow up there and not at all like an eagle or a gull. Fragile, not strong. I think I told her how beautiful the mountains and the valley looked. I didn't tell her how small my house and my brother appeared to me and how my school seemed like a toy building and how that made me want to laugh but also made me sad. I asked her if she had liked it.

"It was educational," she said. "But I think I'll stick to climbing ladders."

The snow keeps falling, a curtain of white that drops across the valley. The crow stays for a while longer in the cottonwood tree, then with a loud cry flaps away to wherever it is crows go when blizzards come. By five o'clock in the afternoon a gray twilight tugs the streetlights on. By eight o'clock the highways are closing. The power goes out as snow-laden lines snap. Thick branches crack under the weight of wet snow. In the dark we listen to the battery-operated radio tuned to a Denver talk show station that calls itself the blowtorch of the Rocky Mountain West because of its wide range of broadcast area. People call in to chat about the storm; most are excited newcomers from California. What feather merchants. My husband and I laugh at them and shake our heads.

But inside we are as excited as they. This is childhood again, feeling the wind trying to rip the house apart but knowing that it will stand; hoping the snow won't stop falling until it is six feet deep; listening enthralled to the litany of road closures, and especially school closures, on the radio. It's worth the inconvenience of a blizzard just to relive that excitement and awe at the power of the natural world.

But the cottonwoods, I'm afraid, may not leaf out this year. Their curled green buds are frozen, and the willow branches have turned gray.

*T*HUNDER *H*OOF *W*IND

Spring

THE WORD "SPRING" in Wyoming means "snow." Formerly a constant companion, the westerly wind weakens and slips away. Gulf air masses stampede north in its place. This wind is known worldwide under different aliases: *siffanto* in Italy; *kai* in China; *vendavales* in Spain. Here its name is thunder hoof wind, the fence flattener.

Between rain showers one spring, shortly before we left Laramie, I celebrated the changing of the season by driving out to see Mr. Kay, a buffalo rancher north of town, bringing along our firstborn son, Adam, who was one at the time. I was writing for an agribusiness weekly and had been sent to see what running a buffalo operation was like on the Laramie Plains.

We drove north to a two-second blink on the road, Bosler. Turning west as directed, we headed across a great green bowl of grass. We drove for miles on the hard-packed dirt road but no matter how fast or how far I drove, the mountains on the other side of the Laramie Basin seemed no closer. Nervous, I wondered if I'd taken the wrong cutoff. Mr. Kay had said to look for trees, but none were in sight for miles. Maybe I'd come the wrong way. Maybe, the shy person's refrain, I shouldn't have come at all. Then I saw it—a dark smudge on the side of a low hill. House, outbuildings, and a few trees soon emerged from the shadowed area like a bronze bas-relief. On the hilltop dark shapes moved slowly across the prairie. Too tall to be cattle, too bulky to be horses, they were, I realized, buffalo.

Such stubborn, mythic, mysterious creatures the American bison are, these prairie hulks more commonly known as buffalo. Symbol of the old West, both savior and Achilles heel to the Plains Indians who depended on its meat and by-products, buffalo roamed the treeless land like a huge, dark cloud shadow. When the white men began their systematic slaughter of the buffalo, further endangering the tribes that depended on the herds for sustenance, it must have at first seemed impossible to imagine that an animal as common as a flea would become nearly extinct. But as the slaughter continued, so their population waned, as did the strength and numbers of the Plains tribes. An age-old method of extinguishing a people entails destroying their source of food. Whether burning crops in medieval Europe or killing buffalo in frontier America, the result was the same. A people's livelihood, and independence, was destroyed.

But the buffalo have come back. In national parks and on private lands, buffalo roam protected and some ranchers find them a viable alternative to raising cattle. Health-conscious consumers prize the animal for its lean, low-cholesterol meat. A top-producing buffalo bull can command a price of tens of thousands of dollars at the National Western Stock Show in Denver, as breeders seek quality bloodlines. I had to remember that at least for my readers, the importance of the buffalo today was the market value of its hide and meat, rather than the more nebulous emotional and historical value I attached to it.

Though often seen as sheepish and slow as any domestic cow, buffalo can be quick and unpredictable, their sharp horns ready to gore the unsuspecting human who ventures too close. I didn't know about this until long after Mr. Kay and I had walked among one of his herds. As I pulled up to the house, he walked out to greet me. He was shorter than me by half a foot, skinnier, too. His legs were slightly bowed out from his years as a ranch hand when every day was spent on a horse. His dark gray hair formed crisp waves and his skin looked like shellacked pine. If a hungry coyote ever got hold of this carcass, he'd have a tough chew.

Yet his eyes were bright, intelligent, and friendly. He offered me coffee black as petroleum, which I sipped in scalding swallows. My son sat quietly on my lap staring at Mr. Kay, who offered him a glass of water. I tried not to look the tenderfoot I was, but I'm sure he could tell I wasn't ranch born, nor an experienced journalist. After all, what real-life reporter ever had the naiveté to bring her one-year-old son along? Finally, with a sense of relief on both our parts, we climbed into Kay's old pickup. Stopping at a pre-fab building, Kay went in and reappeared with a burlap sack filled with hard, shiny blocks of feed that looked like green ice cubes. It smelled sweet and crumbled slightly in my hands, like cake. "Cake," in fact, was what Kay called it.

As we clattered along on a tooth-loosening dirt road up the hill behind the house, Kay relaxed a bit and I asked him why he'd chosen to raise buffalo. He talked about the market value of the meat and hides.

Prices were high but trucking the animals out wasn't easy. One guy he knew had tried to ship a load of buffalo but the animals demolished the cattle truck before it had even left the ranch. He ventured to add that their independence and intelligence (and demolishing a cattle truck was a sign of both) were greater than that of cattle, and that therefore buffalo were less of an economic risk. For example, he said, cattle could starve in winter, not being smart enough to paw through the snow to look for grass, but buffalo did not starve. They were survivors, canny and tough. In the end he finally concluded, "I guess I just like buffalo."

We drove toward the middle of nowhere, unraveling tire tracks behind us in the dirt. The house had disappeared to the south of us, and the interstate lay somewhere to the west. Further to the south lay Laramie, I knew, but all I saw in that direction was an arc of blue sky and prairie ending in sparkling white Colorado mountain tops. Kay stopped the truck to show me a conventional barbed wire fence that had been toppled by one of the two herds he owned. First one buffalo would feel the urge to jump over the fence, whether for food, for water, or just to be ornery, who knows. It would jump, might even clear the top—quite a feat for such a bulky short-legged creature—and land safely on the other side. Other buffalo, watching, would decide to follow, but not quite clearing the fence, their bodies would brush it as they landed, causing it to lean. The rest of the herd would see the leaning fence and run over it, finishing the flattening process. A flattened fence is a fence in name only, hence Kay's fences were constructed of thick four-foot-tall posts and heavy wire.

One spring, Kay said, a pregnant buffalo jumped and rammed her way through a series of cattle fences to find the place where she wanted to drop her calf. The entire herd tagged along behind her until she reached her destination, miles to the west near the interstate. A trail of flattened fences showed their path. Why she had to go to that particular place, no different from others on the ranch, Kay didn't know, yet there was a note of admiration in his voice as he told the story. Perhaps such stubborn determination appealed to him. Perhaps the triumph of sheer instinct spoke to him. Or maybe it was what he would have called just plain cussedness.

We were still searching for the herds as we drove. The sky turned gray and the character of the land seemed to change too, becoming colorless and less benign. Bouncing up a hill, the truck then descended into a depression on the other side, a cupped curve in the land. Just room enough for a stock tank and windmill. And a small herd of buffalo.

They were milling around the water like par-tygoers around a punchbowl. Dark heads turned; small black eyes stared at the truck. As if on cue, they began to sidle toward us like shy yet curious children. They were bigger than I had imagined, with huge backs and ridiculously small hind legs. Strips of red-brown winter fur hung from their coats in shreds. Their shiny, thick black horns looked as sharp as icepicks.

Kay let the truck roll to a gentle stop and opened the door. "Ever fed a buffalo?" he asked, digging in the sack for some cubes of cake.

"No," I said. I wasn't sure I wanted to start now. My son, who had sat quietly throughout the day, placed his hands on the dashboard and bounced on the seat as a few edged nearer to the truck, pretending to be busy nibbling grass.

"He better stay here," Kay said. Trusting him, and the stars that have watched over many of my stupid actions, I grabbed my camera, got out, opened the window a crack, patted my son, and closed the door.

Kay gave me a handful of sweet cubes, which I shoved in my coat pocket. As he walked off a few yards from the truck and offered some cake on the flat of his hand to one hornless yearling, I shot pictures with the old Mamiya 35-millimeter camera, hoping this wouldn't be the day it finally quit working.

Ripples of movement in the herd showed we were attracting stragglers from the edge; they were joining the braver insiders who'd followed the truck. From the corner of my eye I saw brown clouds gathering.

"How's about I take a picture of you now?" Kay asked. He hadn't liked being photographed. I handed him the camera and took some cake from my pocket. I had just time enough to point out the shutter release before a woolly reddish-brown mass as big as a Volkswagen stepped over. I glimpsed a fat pink tongue and a tiny black eye looking at me and felt its warm breath on my hand before the creature moved off to munch the sweet food.

A few minutes later, having hand-fed some of the more daring and hungry of the herd, we climbed back, ungored, into the truck and were welcomed by my little boy. Kay steered the pickup slowly through the herd until the buffalo were left behind. I pulled out my notepad, ready to ask some more questions.

As the pickup bounced across the little valley, Kay rolled down his window and glanced in the rearview mirror. "Look behind you," he said.

I turned around. The herd was trotting after us.

Kay gunned the engine and sped up. I heard a low rumbling sound. The herd was running, pounding after us, chasing the truck they knew carried food.

We careened up and over a hill. The buffalo disappeared. The rumbling stopped.

"Hell of a lot smarter than cows," said Kay.

Back at the house again, our awkwardness returned. Kay mentioned almost casually his legal troubles with water rights. Someone was suing him for use of some of his water, in the "use it or lose it" world of western water rights. It all went over my head and into the sky. I was still flying across the land with a herd of buffalo thundering after me. I couldn't wait to get home, develop the film, and tell my husband about it.

Now, more than a decade later, as the boy who accompanied me listens to this story that is pure myth to him, I wish I had asked Kay more questions. Different questions, about water rights and how they can be lost, and what this loss means in a semi-arid land where the winds suck all the moisture from the grasses and trees. What it means in economic, as well as personal terms.

But I think that's why I didn't ask. Kay seemed injured by what was happening to him, and I didn't want to make it worse. I wasn't much of a journalist on that day and I didn't much care. On that day I was a young woman an old man could show his herd of buffalo to, and in witnessing her delight and awe, forget the worries pressing down on him.

I don't know what happened to him or his buffalo or his ranch. Park of me doesn't want to know the conclusion. That way the coffee is still hot, the cake is still sweet, the water flows into the stock tank like sparkling punch, and the buffalo are always thundering after his pickup truck.

❧ ❧ ❧

In Wyoming, spring is a capricious season, playing cat-and-mouse games with human hopes. One day crocuses bloom. The next day blizzards blow petals of snow. Beneath the surface of snow and earth the mechanisms of life move upward. Roots stir, pushing the alkaline soil. A shadow of green appears on the land, shifts, disappears when stared at. But I know this much: the cottonwoods didn't lose their young leaves, and the willows are still alive.

In the spring I remember the flowering of an early, hope-filled project: a small weekly newspaper Curt and I started in our early twenties. For me, May is still the month of fresh white paper, green hopes, and the sharp odor of printer's ink. Even now when I walk past a printing shop and smell the ink, I am transported back to a dusty downtown street in Torrington, out on the eastern plains of Wyoming.

I remember how the spring breeze grazed in the cottonwoods, fattened over the lush sod farms as we drove into Torrington. With Adam in tow, a toddler at the time, I walked out of the stuffy office of the *Torrington Telegraph* to escape the noise of the printing press, leaving Curt with the pressman to monitor the printing of our newspaper. We crossed the street to the local doughnut shop, where the woman at the counter still refused to take my out-of-town check, even though we'd been coming every Thursday for months to print our paper, the *Laramie Chronicle*, on the *Telegraph's* press. To her, we would always be strangers. I counted out the price of two longjohns, paying in pennies and nickels. That was all the cash I had and there was only a little more left in our checking account. I was twenty-one years old and looking bankruptcy in the face.

But my boy distracted me. As farmers and ranchers filed in, crowding around Formica tables to sip their morning coffee and jaw about crops and calves, Adam struggled to eat the longjohn. Too late I realized I should have bought him a plain cake doughnut. Mothering was still new to me and I hadn't learned to anticipate these details.

However, I was able to think ahead about the *Chronicle,* and the future I saw worried me. Although only in its infancy, our newspaper was doomed.

That's what I thought, even at the beginning. Every week, I was certain our enterprise was about to fold. But my husband didn't share my fears. Plowing onward, he threw himself into each week's edition, looking beyond the mounting bills and long hours to that future day when we would turn a profit. My pessimism disturbed him—he thought it meant I didn't believe in him. But I was merely facing the facts: the recession had a chokehold on Wyoming; we had little capital and less experience; our competitor was a hundred-year-old daily with a fat bank account and a quaint name folklorists drooled over. The *Boomerang* wasn't about to yield any ground to an upstart rag.

But I ask myself now, as I look back, why couldn't I have believed in our newspaper? Just one shining moment of belief. I had believed in a few choice things in the two decades I'd been on earth: the love of my family, the wisdom of Nasim, the necessity of open space, the malevolence of the wind, the magic of books, the unpredictable cruelty of schoolmates. If I had added to this list "the success of the *Laramie Chronicle,*" would it have made a difference in the end?

It might have.

On that tart green morning in eastern Wyoming, I wavered between belief and doubt. Fields that had worn ugly brown for months now were suddenly lush and green. The air seemed to soften. New life stirred even within my own body—a child, a second son, would arrive in the harsh darkness of the next new year. Why couldn't I have believed for one moment?

The aromas of tomato soup, grilled cheese sandwiches, and cabbage-hamburger rolls called bierocks, wafted from the doughnut kitchen as we left. It was too soon to return to the newspaper office. The press would still be running, the smell of the ink made me sick, and it wasn't a safe place for a little boy. Open cans of chemicals and two-hundred-pound rolls of newsprint propped against the wall awaited his touch the moment my back was turned. Instead we strolled the downtown streets until we reached a park.

Sunlight shot through dark clouds, then disappeared, then reappeared brilliantly, as if someone had flicked a switch. A slide on the other side of the park caught Adam's eye. It was coated with mud. After wiping off what I could, I let his corduroy overalls do the rest as he slowly slid down. His face was serious. This wasn't play.

The wind came back. Land and sky turned gray. The town seemed to have been emptied of all souls and we were alone on a gray planet. I shivered. What would become of us? This was not what I had imagined myself doing three years before as a senior in high school. Frightened, I grabbed my boy and began walking back. But no landmarks stood out among the dead-looking trees and barren homes. Had we come this way or not? Tired, Adam began to cry, mirroring my feelings. I shifted him to my other hip. We were lost, lost in a small town one could drive through in minutes.

Then I heard Nasim's crisp voice: "In that case, just walk faster and either you'll find what you're looking for or you'll reach the edge of town." It revived me. Soon we found the downtown block and ducked into the comforting warmth and clatter of the *Telegraph* office. The women at the counter ignored me, but I decided that meant I belonged there on a Thursday morning. Through doors marked "Authorized Personnel Only" we walked into the pressroom. The double garage doors stood open at the rear, our small green Ford Granada beside them. Curt and another man were loading bundles of newspapers into the car.

I touched a stack, still warm from the press. The front-page photograph looked good. So many of our previous photographs had screened muddy gray, amateurish and ugly, but this one was rich with contrast: deep blacks and silvery whites that Ansel Adams himself might have loved. A good omen, I thought.

I buckled Adam into his carseat and helped the men load the last bundles. When we were finished, the trunk and rear seat were full. Even the space beneath Adam's carseat held a stack of papers. On the floor beneath my feet we stuffed the last bundle. The smell of ink was strong in the car, scenting the upholstery, our clothes, and our hair.

"Any more and you'd have to leave the little guy here," the pressman said as he slammed the door. "Don't break an axle, now."

Slowly we turned out of the alley, tailpipe scraping concrete, and onto the main road. Ahead of us lay a two-hour drive south to Cheyenne, and then an hour drive west to Laramie. This was our chance to rest before the next stage, delivery, began. We hadn't slept since the night before last, having worked feverishly all day and night to meet our printing deadline.

Adam fussed awhile, then fell asleep. One worry out of the way. For the moment, our car was the only one on the highway. As we swooped down a hill, our load pushed us up to seventy-five miles an hour. Maybe this was the best way to avoid feeling lost—go fast. Go faster. Eighty miles an hour, gliding past fields of green sod. The sun came out and warmed us. The car did not break an axle. I leaned back. For the moment, we were safe. And more importantly, I believed it.

LITTLE VERDIGRIS WIND

*Late spring,
hesitant beginning of summer*

⮾ Many Mays have passed and our newspaper no longer warrants even a line on my resume to account for that year. A few copies of the first and last issues, and our accounts book, rest in a box beneath the stairs. Our children ask, "Did you really own a newspaper once?"

Huge cloud shadows darken the burgeoning green slopes of the Laramie Mountains. A soft south wind turns a razor edge, scours the coppery dirt out by the old quarry east of town and lays a coating of pale green vegetation on the prairie. The Little Verdigris wind has come, and though the grasses have been preparing to surge with a blast of green, the wind, alternately warm and cold, heralds their appearance. I am on my way—again—to the neighborhood where my special circle of rock had nestled into a hill. Our search the previous year had been fruitless, but I want another chance just to make sure.

Once again, I feel alien on these new streets where hundreds of people have established themselves. But curiosity wins. I drive north, turn east, north again, east again, north, east, then south. One vacant lot. I slow down. Yes, above the vacant lot, behind someone's backyard, behind piles of broken concrete slabs and crusty stones, a familiar curve of rock hugs the hill. Ignoring the neighborhood watch signs, I stop and stare, then wish I hadn't found it. Less painful was the belief that my most precious haunt was already gone. More painful now is to see it being engulfed by houses and yards, a cancer of runaway growth.

The tires leave rubber on the pavement as I peel out. It was a mistake to come.

∿ ∿ ∿

A storm is moving in from the southeast, not the source of storms for most locales. But our weather often defies expectation, influenced by the nearby mountains. Actually many storms come into the Laramie Basin from the southeast.

It happens like this: like water running in a ditch, a cold wind flows south along the east side of the Laramie Mountains toward Cheyenne. At a low point south of Interstate 80 and east of Highway 287, the wind leaves its channel and spills over into the Laramie Basin. It pours across the valley, flowing north by northwest. Hitting Laramie, it curves westward and heads for the village of Centennial. But the low area along the Laramie River channel causes it to change directions again; it flows along the river, heading northeast to Wheatland, through a cut in the Laramie Mountains and out onto the eastern plains again in a huge clockwise circle.

If the winds wore colors, as the Irish myths say, what a curlicue of color would stream in and around these mountains and across this valley.

Near the end of June, the cyclonic storms and strong winds of winter dissipate. Moist air begins to push up from the south. Afternoon skies darken as thunderstorms reproduce and mother clouds give birth to more clouds. One morning in late June, when I was eleven or twelve, my father and brother and I walked across the prairie and up the long broad back of the Laramie Mountains. We followed an old dirt road. Our goal: the summit of Pilot Knob. Halfway up the mountain, we stopped at a small gully rimmed by scrawny lodgepole pines and ate our lunch of tuna fish sandwiches and sweet cherries. My brother found an antelope horn, black and curved like a scimitar. We passed a sheepherder's wagon, a miniature tin-roofed cart just big enough for a man to take shelter in on a cold rainy night. But there was no man and there were no sheep. As we walked farther and farther from home, I began to feel uneasy. Looking back, I could make out the town, which appeared like a narrow dark blue shadow down in the valley; our house was a tiny chip of yellow in the mosaic of houses that was our neighborhood. Here and there a glint of metal flashed—sunlight reflecting off cars on the highway. Up here, nothing moved. Everything was quiet.

We hiked across sheets of tan rock that looked as though once they'd flowed as molten lava. The summit of Pilot Knob was still hours away. Then we heard thunder. Feeling vulnerable on the exposed sheet of rock, we turned around and jogged back down the road, reaching the pine-rimmed gully as the wind came up and the first drops flew. Snapping together a couple of ponchos, we huddled together on the side of the gully, sheltered from the wind by sagebrush. There, we ate the remaining cherries as the rain spat and the storm began in earnest. Lightning crackled around us and thunder hammered. Now the rain came in sheets of nails, pounding our poncho in short, violent bursts. Minutes later, the storm was over. Emerging, we sniffed the sweet sage-filled air.

We never made it up Pilot Knob. A rancher drove by in his pickup truck and we hitched a ride back to town. At home an hour later, I sat at my desk by the windows overlooking the prairie and tracked how far we'd gone up the mountain. Half a pencil's length. I wrote in my steno notebook, journal number three, about the tuna fish, cherries, storm, horn, and pines. Rereading it over twenty years later, I see no mention of my lost feeling just before the storm. Reflecting now, I think perhaps that's because the lost feeling was too confusing for me to explore. After all, there I'd been with my big, strong dad, and my competent little brother, out hiking the mountain I gazed at every day from my bedroom window. I was safe, I was doing what I loved, with people I loved, and yet I'd suddenly realized that the world was truly bigger than I was, that what seemed near was really far, that hazards and pleasures shared equal billing.

I was not one to respond to the landscape with logic. If I saw a strange bird, I could not identify it, nor did I care to, as the act of learning someone else's nomenclature for the birds of my lovely prairie world was not satisfying. Yes, I picked up names from Nasim and from others around me, such as the western meadowlark, the starling, the sparrow. But making my own names was more satisfying. Hence the meadowlark, for me, was really the yellow-breast-throat-ripple bird, and the starling was the streak of purple-jet-black-oily bird. Grasses growing on the prairie I defined by their appearance as well: some had woven ends, others had needle-like ends, others had tips shaped like half-moons. Flowers and rocks, too, I defined by appearance, not by Latin words or names of male scientists. I was a scientific illiterate, unable to read the landscape around me.

ᐁ ᐁ ᐁ

Fast-forward to another hike, only the little brother is a research professor and the big sister is his temporary field assistant filling in between graduate students. We climb out of Mark's truck on a dirt road somewhere northeast of Jackson Lake, in Grand Teton National Park in northwestern Wyoming. Shrugging on our packs on this warm July morning, we velcro the bear mace cans to our belts, and strike out for the pathless forest where we are going to extract tree ring samples as part of his NASA grant to study forestation. As we cut across the rough forests and meadows, he checks our position with a global positioning satellite device the size of his palm, then verifies on two contour maps where we are headed. We keep up a chatter of conversation so as to warn any bears of our presence. This is, after all, bear country, though the only signs of bears have been human ones posted on the roads and trailheads warning us of their imminent appearance. However, several other researchers at the University of Wyoming Research Station have reported encounters with bears in the past week.

As we hike up and over numerous ridges, I peer from the crest of one and see an oblong blue puddle spread beneath the jagged peaks of the Tetons: Jackson Lake. If not for that landmark, I wouldn't have a clue where we are. As I follow my brother down the other side of the ridge on his complicated route to the site he has chosen to sample, I wonder if I would be able to find my way back through the tangle of wilderness if something happened to him. I see how the global positioning device works but doubt I could match it up to the map's coordinates precisely enough to find my way back. Nervously, I pay closer attention to the turns he makes, playing them in reverse in my brain, sorting out the details we pass and imprinting them as landmarks: that creek with the eroded high bank: remember it. That old rusty-orange carcass of a Douglas fir tree leaning half-fallen across the forest canopy: remember it. That marshy little meadow, full of stalks of purple fireweed: remember it. They are the keys to my way out of this maze.

We walk around a pile of fresh coyote scat—at least that's what my brother says it is when I worriedly point it out. So far we've only seen the little black jelly-beans of elk droppings in the meadows near the creek, but no other signs of the presence of wildlife, probably because of our deliberate loudness. Mark assures me that coyotes don't normally have anything to do with humans and I don't pause to wonder why coyotes would stray into this dense forest from the sagebrush flatlands where I've seen them before. I should know better. This is the same brother who assured me, as he coaxed me to walk out to the middle of a rickety rail-road trestle spanning the high gorge of Letchworth State Park in western New York, that trains didn't use that route anymore. Minutes later, I heard a train whistle and we clutched the shaky wooden railing as a freight train thundered by three feet away from us.

But I take his word and believe in the errant coyote. We reach the sampling site, which appears to be a chunk of forest similar to much of the forest we've already walked through, comprised mainly of various conifers growing as high as telephone poles, with so many fallen logs that walking is more like a scramble across rungs of a ladder than a stroll across flat ground.

First he measures off the square we will work within. It is large enough that when I stand at one cor-ner, I can't see him at the opposite corner, though we can hear each other. He hustles along each side, calling out names of trees and writing them in his field notebook. Some of the names I recognize, such as Douglas fir. Others I do not. His camera whirrs softly as he photographs the site. My job is to carry gear and to follow him around, and though he does not say it, my job is also to keep a watch out for bears. I look like a speed-crazed junkie, I'm sure, as I stand nervously poised, head jerking this way, that way, eyes wide open, ready to scream at the slightest crackle of paw on pine needle. For each tree he samples, he first estimates the height, explaining to me, as if my brain is really working, how he does it using simple mathematics. But my brain is in survival mode. I nod, dumbly, saving my voice for when the bears come. He hands me the notebook and I record the numbers he calls out.

Then he takes a little auger to his sample tree's trunk, pierces it, then removes a perfect little cream and brown cross-section of the tree's trunk, and slips it into a drinking straw, which he caps at both ends with masking tape, then labels according to his numbering system for categorizing the trees within this site. This is done for every tree of a certain diameter within the sampling area, a chore which takes several hours to complete.

Now and then the chattering of squirrels and the chirping of birds suddenly stills, and we both stop what we are doing and scan the forest quickly. If we have been silent for a while, I start to talk, babbling questions about the trees, the wildflowers, so that any bears roaming the forest will hear and, if they are normal bears, will avoid our section and browse for food elsewhere. My brother rattles off the scientific as well as common names of all the flowers and trees in the area as if they are his good friends, and suddenly I see what I've been missing as a scientific illiterate: he's on a first-name basis with everything that grows here in this national park, whether it's in this coniferous ecosystem, or the riparian ecosystem of the river valley further south, or the sagebrush flats to the southeast, or the alpine ecosystem of the glacial hanging lakes he hikes to on his days off. This national park is his Prairie now.

After a quick snack and some water, we pack up the equipment and start back down. Because my voice suddenly feels hoarse, and I've run out of questions to ask him, I begin to sing, as I am certain any bear would run immediately from my singing voice. As we cross a meadow through waist-high grasses, my brother in the lead, something erupts from under Mark's boots and he yells and jumps backward, then starts to laugh. A brown blur crashes across the meadow and dodges into the forest. No bear. Just an elk calf, hidden in the deep meadow grasses, which Mark nearly stepped on.

He examines his map again and runs his finger down a different section of the contours to show the way we're headed. He's found a shortcut back, though it will be steep. I'm game.

We bushwhack across hillsides of fallen trees and scratchy brush, down a heavily shaded creek, cut across more wet, spongy meadows and into shadowed forests, until suddenly, we're on the rough path where we had begun. It is late afternoon now as we peel off our dusty, sweat-darkened packs and climb into his truck. As we drive back to the research station I admit how nervous I'd been about encountering a bear and how surprised I am that we saw none. Then he mentions the coyote scat. It wasn't really coyote scat, he tells me. It was bear scat. Fresh too. Most likely a bear had been in that area at about the same time we had.

"I didn't want to make you more nervous by telling you what it really was," he said.

Oh, being a scientific illiterate may have its benefits after all.

～ ～ ～

Recently I went out walking on the prairie, surrounded only by miles of blue grama and buffalo grass. Above, cumulus clouds sailed eastward, moving with the dignity of clipper ships. The wind rumbled in my ears. I stepped over a line of piled rocks onto a smooth piece of prairie, closed my eyes and spun around until the rumble became a dull hum.

When I opened my eyes, I was standing at the center of a wide polygon of grass bounded by ankle-high piles of rocks that formed a low border on the rough ground. A magic circle, my younger self would have said. My adult self was silent. No explanations. It was as if a giant broom had swept the stones into piles, leaving bare grass in the middle. It didn't look natural. But what human would travel out to this unexceptional piece of ground in the Laramie Basin and clear out these areas of grass? Sheepherders, I thought, remembering the stone shafts Nasim and I had searched for. But no, sheepherders wouldn't risk having their sheep break their legs on these rock borders. Cowboys? Native Americans? Visitors from outer space? Or maybe these are ancient archaeological relics, the remains of a people who lived in many-sided houses of stone thousands of years ago. But no clues exist to reveal their creators' identity.

Later I learned that nature creates such polygons in a quiet, slow process involving water, ice, and gravity. During a thaw, moisture seeps into small cracks in rocks, and when the moisture freezes, it expands like a wedge, causing the rocks to fracture. Moisture also creeps beneath the surface of the soil and expands as it freezes, causing the ground to rise in places. As these frost heaves occur, rocks roll to lower areas where they begin gradually to collect, surrounding the bare higher ground in a polygon-like shape.

Scientists call such a sight "patterned ground." From the air the lines of piled rocks seem to form cells with grassy interiors and rocky outlines. Sometimes the stone polygons are shaped into circles, which scientists think has to do with concentrations of clay in the soil and the circulation of water beneath the surface. My disappointment in learning that these shapes were not arranged by ancient human hands changed to amazement that a simple action of temperature change could cause such patterns of rock to form. Here, daily, through the winters and springs of thousands of years, countless small adjustments when the climate was colder and wetter had arranged these rocks into what scientists call "fossil ice-wedge polygons." Maybe I was not so far off in calling them magic circles after all.

When I least expect it, patterns emerge. Small actions, seemingly random, can, if multiplied by thousands, result in a design. Sometimes we just need to stand back and refocus to see it. Look at any photograph under a microscope and the image is reduced to pixels, the tiny units of light and shadow that, individually, mean nothing to the human eye. But step back from the photograph and the pixels combine into a pattern, a recognizable image.

Sometimes I think a dual way of seeing is necessary to fully appreciate the intricacies of our planet. Seeing the Douglas fir forest, as well as the individual forty-year-old tree. Finding mystery in polygonal outlines of rocks dotting the prairie, yet appreciating the scientific explanation for their creation. Noting the details of each precious moment of life, yet remembering that human time is a mere pixel in the universe's giant still-developing photograph.

But if I know one thing, I know why I'm here, on the prairie, at high noon in the wind and sunlight. I'm here so the wind will have something to push against, so the sun will have something to peel besides tough sagebrush leaves and dry soil. So the antelope on the other side of the barbed wire fence will have something to flee from.

I see four at a distance. A cup of land separates us, as well as a few hundred yards of grass and sagebrush. The animals' delicate legs can hardly be seen, but the patches of white on belly and rump stand out. The human eye fills in the details. Antelope look like fragile, stick animals when seen in the scale of the huge grassy land and blue dome of sky, but they were made just for wide-open spaces like this. They want no trees or shrubs cluttering their line of sight, as they depend on their keen vision to spot predators, and they need miles of open ground through which to run at speeds of up to sixty miles an hour. Ironically, hunters have found antelope a ready target, as the animals' curiosity can cause them to stop running to look at a strange, new object, leaving them momentarily vulnerable.

Nasim showed me the power of antelope vision on a hike with my Girl Scout troop. The troop leader had arranged for Nasim to lead us out on the prairie west of Tie Siding, as we were all working on our hiking and camping badges at the time. As we scuffed along behind her, chattering and giggling, she suddenly stopped and told us to hush. "The prairie ghost," she hissed. That quieted us for a moment. She pointed in the distance but I saw nothing. Then she passed around two powerful pairs of binoculars. "This is how far they can see. They're looking at you now."

When one of the pairs made it to my hands, I looked through the lenses and didn't want to put them down. My thick eyeglasses had nothing on her binoculars. I saw the texture of each grass blade, the fuzziness of each sagebrush leaf, each rib and curve and nub of rabbitbrush. Then I saw them: the antelope herd. I saw the hairs on their sun-browned ginger coats, the shine of their black horns. Several looked up, gazed across the distance into my binoculars and for one long moment I thought they looked into me. I barely breathed. But suddenly one turned, as if it had been the sentinel, and its white rump hairs lifted, signaling danger to the others. They turned and ran. The girl who'd just gotten the other binoculars groaned and my friend nudged me, wanting her turn. I handed her the binoculars and told her the antelope had gone. She checked to be sure, then handed the binoculars back and followed the other girls who were trailing Nasim as she strode over to a gopher hole to show them something else. I stayed behind, scanning the prairie with the powerful lenses, pretending I was an antelope.

Like other mammals in the American West, the pronghorn antelope was misnamed by English-speaking settlers. It is not an antelope but the sole member of its own family, *Antilocapridae.* True antelopes live in Asia and Africa.

The jackrabbit, colleague of the antelope, was also misnamed: it is actually not a rabbit but a hare. One difference between the two is that a hare is born strong, eyes open, legs ready to run. A newborn rabbit, on the other hand, is blind and helpless. A notable difference if one is a rabbit.

Another misnomer, the prairie dog is a ground squirrel that lives in a network of branching tunnels, the negative-space opposite of tree limbs. Some say they were so named because of their high-pitched call of alarm, which to early travelers sounded like a bark. Few of those early travelers thought much of the prairie dog. Walter Prescott Webb, in *The Great Plains,* quotes Colonel Richard I. Dodge: "I regard the prairie dog as a machine designed by nature to convert grass into flesh, and thus furnish the proper food to the carnivora of the plain…." Some of the people I grew up with would rephrase Colonel Dodge: "I regard the prairie dog as a machine designed for target practice…."

Even land managers with lofty goals of preserving ecosystems sometimes regard the prairie dog as a species less than worthy. In some protected ecosystems, prairie dogs have been moved or poisoned by the very organizations devoted to preserving wildlife because these rodents' burrowing habit caused erosion that threatened the entire ecosystem.

The black-footed ferret once helped control prairie dog populations by roaming their tunnels and feeding on them. But the black-footed ferret is nearly extinct. Coyotes, too, used to help control prairie dogs, as did hawks and prairie falcons. But the presence of humans has controlled those populations, while prairie dogs proliferate.

In Colorado, management of precious wild lands at the edges of the metropolitan Denver corridor becomes more difficult not only as certain species flourish at the expense of others, but also because management methods endure close scrutiny by a public that often lives right beside the open space. Recently one county was contacted by a resident who threatened to blanket a protected area with protest leaflets unless the wildlife managers stopped the prairie dog "control." They labeled him simplistic, emotional, crazy. Didn't he realize that the spread of prairie dog burrows on one parcel of land threatened the whole ecosystem with erosion? Another parcel of land had been set aside specifically for prairie dogs, so what was the big deal if they were moved to that area? And if that parcel couldn't support such a large number of prairie dogs, well, then the population would have to be "controlled" but it was for a greater good: the preservation of an entire ecosystem.

He didn't buy it, but maybe they told him the fine for littering and he decided to protest in some other way.

I waver between the wildlife managers and the leaflet man. Some days I agree with the wildlife managers. I compare their hold on the environment to that of an emergency-room nurse's hands on a patient—gentle but unyielding for the patient's own good. Once when my oldest son was an infant, we took him to the hospital as we feared he had a bowel obstruction. The emergency room nurse asked that I hold Adam firmly on the examining table so that he could be diagnosed. As he began to cry, I eased up, and the nurse pushed me aside. She then held him down with great firmness and he was quickly examined and treated. My tender, loving arms were no help to him. In the same way, wildlife managers have a firm hold on the ecosystems they are supposed to maintain and protect. Though a tenderhearted public finds their methods cruel, such methods can sometimes accomplish the long-term goal of preserving the ecosystem.

But other days I want to run outside with the leaflet man and shout against the killing of these prairie dogs, these golden-brown, rotund rodents who have the nerve to do what they've been programmed to do, which is to dig and burrow. How could they know the land they've chosen is protected, even from themselves? I want to follow the leaflet man as he flings a blizzard of paper across the prairie and see if what he does solves any problems. But I know it won't. Like the wildlife managers he abhors, his actions, though based on love of the land and its animals, would cause more problems. Besides, like the well-trained daughter and mother I am, I'd probably start picking up after him. Oh love will get you into trouble no matter what.

It seems you would not be a good wildlife resource manager, the antelopes say, as they turn and look across the polygon-studded prairie at me.

Let me run with you, I plead.

No, they answer. Your love is not enough.

And in a minute they're a mile gone.

FIRE EYES WIND

Early summer

ON SUMMER MORNINGS, my brother Mark and I liked to get up early and cook breakfast out on the prairie. We'd bring an old coffee can, the largest available, with a hole cut in one side, a tuna fish can with paraffin and cardboard packed inside as a makeshift source of fuel, matches, eggs, margarine, and pancake batter in a plastic bottle. On a patch of bare dirt we'd set the tuna can down and light the paraffin and cardboard inside it, then put the coffee can, bottom up, cut side downwind, on top of it to make a small stove. When the coffee can got hot, we'd slice a pat of margarine and let it sizzle on the can, then crack eggs onto the can and watch them fry.

We'd bask in the sun, the wind a gentle finger stroking our heads, while meadowlarks sang their liquid songs. Everyone else was asleep as we sat back on our heels and ate undercooked egg and pancake with our fingers and sniffed the burning paraffin and cardboard. Then the wind would come up, squirting dust in our eyes, lashing our little fire; someone's lawn mower would kick into action far off, we'd hear cars rumbling on distant roads, and a jet would scratch a white line in the blue sky overhead. Time to go. The rest of the world was now awake.

One such morning, however, the wind didn't kick up. After our breakfast all was quiet except for the meadowlarks. I opened the field guide to flowers that I'd borrowed from Nasim and attempted to find the name of a red flower on a silvery green stem growing near my boot. Thumbing page after page, I soon became bored. Nothing on paper seemed to match the reality of stem and petal. I put down the book and decided to return it to Nasim later.

But "later" kept receding until a year had gone by and the field guide was still on my bookshelf gathering dust. The breakfast cookouts with my brother had ended, houses were being built out on the prairie, and my dog was getting fat from lack of exercise. My best friend had her driver's license and now our days were spent dashing around town and on the hills and dirt roads north and east of town in her '48 Willys

Jeep. Who needed to know what wildflower was called by what name, when one had wheels and a license and a clear summer day and miles of road to explore?

It was a wonderful summer, the time of push: flowers, trees, grasses, insects—life in all its forms was pushing to its utmost, pushing to the ends of stems and petals, to the ends of twigs and wings, growing madly in the short time available between spring and fall. That July I could practically feel the straining, like a pit bull terrier lunging at the end of its chain, on the verge of breaking free. Mornings were steeped with the strong smell of sagebrush. Afternoons brought clouds charging across the sky, drenching the land with violent rain showers that ended minutes after they began. Green grass spread like a green fire across the valley; green leaves covered every branch, every stick.

Now, in the time of Fire Eyes, I have finally learned the names of four flowers at least: pasque flower, wild verbena, wild aster, and bluebell. Nasim would have given grudging approval, if she'd known. Then she'd have asked, "What about the other six?" Her advice in spring was, "Count ten kinds of wildflowers blooming to be assured that winter is truly gone."

Following her example, I go out on the prairie alone, with not even a dog for company, as I am between dogs right now. I drive slowly, in a very stodgy car, out past the town dump, on the road to Rogers Canyon. It was there that a girl I knew in high school died when her boyfriend's car slammed into a rock wall as he took a curve too fast. I stop as soon as the town's sprawl is hidden by long, gentle curves of land. But I don't go into the canyon.

Half of me wants to get out and walk, walk far enough that I can feel swallowed up by open land and sky. The other half thinks of a potential news story on the Denver TV stations that evening: "Police say her car was found abandoned on a stretch of road northeast of Laramie…." Why do I long for prairie solitude? Is it my introversion, dating from childhood? My overactive imagination that dreams of cracking open the mysteries of the universe in a single insight? The desire for that fleeting feeling, not often glimpsed now that I'm an adult, of belonging to a place? What if, once I start walking, I don't want to come back to my car?

I compromise: walk ten feet from the car, squat on my heels in a patch of blue grama grass, pretend the asphalt highway isn't so close. A boy in my high school social studies class who went on to live an adventurous life made a comment that I never forgot: by the time you're a grownup, he said, you get the face you deserve. I think I remember that comment because I began to worry: How would my face change? And what kind would I deserve? Would I end up with a frowning, bitter face? An anxious, fearful face?

It is said that an Indonesian god of the winds, Lowalangi, breathes a soul into each person at birth and asks that person what he or she wishes to do with this life. If some of us are wandering around not sure what to do with our lives, maybe we have forgotten our reply to Lowalangi. Another maxim that Nasim told me, but which I've only now begun to understand, is that taking small chances results in a small life. Thinking of this as I sit down on my patch of compromise, I look at my watch and realize that at this very minute, a friend of mine is undergoing surgery. If it fails, she'll be blind. If it succeeds—and the odds are good that it will—she'll be able to toss out her Coke-bottle eyeglasses. We share the same poor vision, but she's doing something about it, taking a chance. I hang back and watch.

The Arapaho tell a story of a man who threw his eyes away into the branches of a cottonwood tree. We are not told if it was an impulsive gesture or one that was pondered for days. But to compensate, he borrowed the eyes of various other animals: coyote, hawk, bear, deer. As he looked through those different lenses, what did he become? Did he become Coyote, learning the prairie's contours from two and a half feet above it, trotting across a crisp field of snow, stomach shrunken, surrounded by light glaring off snow crystals, a cold wind burning his eyes? Become Hawk, watching for the flick of a tail in shifting grass blades a hundred feet away, tightening to coast in circles on an invisible column of rising air, feeling the wind tearing at wing tips? Become Bear, looking for the next familiar shape of chokecherry bush, smelling stories on the wind, lumbering across a rounded hill of bear-shaped bushes?

"Use your eyes," Nasim would say to me, which usually meant I hadn't noticed something I was supposed to. She liked to tell me about the scientist Louis Agassiz, who sent a young scientist back again and again to look at a fish. Each time the young scientist came back with new details to tell of, thinking he had finally seen all there was to see of the fish. Agassiz would send him back to look yet again, beyond the first, the second, the third impressions. Nasim was fond of telling me to look beyond appearances. She used herself as an example. She looked delicate with her finely braided white hair coiled on top of her head, thin wrists and arms, small feet and narrow build. Silver-rimmed glasses dangled from a strand of pearls around her neck, and she favored cardigans of powder blue, flowered housedresses, and shoes of sensible black that buckled across the instep. Her appearance said, "Active in a mainline Christian church, volunteers at the hospital auxiliary gift shop, drives an older model American car. Conservative, predictable."

No one would realize, to look at her, that she'd walked out onto the sagebrush shrubland west of Laramie one morning soon after her husband's death and tried to kill herself. She carried a bottle of his pain pills, three-fourths full, and his old black metal Thermos filled with water. She intended to take a permanent nap out on the prairie where no one would find her body for weeks, maybe months.

She didn't reckon on being found within hours. After the first handful went down, Nasim dropped the bottle of pills, lay down near some sagebrush bushes, and closed her eyes to the morning sunlight. When she woke up at twilight surrounded by a flock of bawling, greasy-wooled sheep, she sat up, nearly giving the Basque sheepherder a heart attack. He recovered quickly enough to call off his dogs as she crouched in the dirt and vomited. He knew hardly any English, so they communicated by gestures. She felt that he was terrified of her; perhaps he thought she was a witch or a ghost. Or perhaps he was afraid of her because she was a woman. She didn't feel like a woman. She felt dried out, with dust for blood, ashes for skin, and a voice full of sand. No life force ran through her body.

The herder made her a tent out of an oily olive green tarp. Nasim stayed for a week near his wagon, eating his food, listening to him sing, and mending the holes in his socks, though he could sew as well as she. And there, in the wind and sun, the sky and sagebrush, she considered what to do with herself. Her husband's pension was small but the house was in good shape and paid off, as were their two cars. She was in good health, scrawny but tough. She had no children, no grandchildren, no nephews, no nieces, no sisters, no brothers, no parents, and now, no spouse. If she thought for long about it, she felt a twinge of terror, but an exhilarating one. For the first time in years she wasn't caring for a spouse, parent, or anyone at all. She could do what she wanted to, instead of tailoring her desires to meet others' needs and expectations. Only what did she want to do?

After a week with the sheepherder, Nasim went home long enough to pick up her husband's old canvas tent and sleeping bag. Her short stay on the land had whetted her taste for more. Gone was the fear of the teenaged girl out winter camping. Sheep Mountain, tall and broad, rising from the floor of the

Laramie Basin—that was her next goal. She'd always wondered what it would be like to stand on its tree-covered shoulders and look out across the Laramie Valley. The sheepherder had drawn her a map of a trail. He didn't tell her it was patrolled by brusque ranch managers on horseback.

As she loaded up the tent and sleeping bag and supplies from her kitchen, her neighbors appeared, concerned about her absence. She told them she'd been to visit an old friend who was near death. They doubtless imagined some blue-haired respectable old lady, and Nasim realized her age and appearance could be used as a disguise. She could do what she wanted, as long as the rest of the town saw only the churchgoing, volunteering, sensible-oxfords, pearl-necklace old lady.

And what did she want? She wanted to tramp around the mountains and learn the names of things. She wanted to draw and paint what she saw and have the result be recognizable. She wanted to write poetry, even if it was terrible, and study biology, even if she didn't entirely understand it. She wanted to dig for dinosaur bones and volunteer to hide Central American refugees in her house. She wanted to dance under the full moon in the middle of nowhere. She wanted to know the stories of everything. She would use her public name as a shield, the name that could have been Doris, or Jeannette, or Betty, or Rayleen, the name that revealed nothing about her true self and everything about her parents' taste in female names, and she would rename herself, privately. She chose an Arabic word for a seasonal desert wind: Nasim.

I had met her as Doris-Jeanette-Betty-Rayleen. Mrs. Sands. I came to know her as Nasim after I'd looked beyond the shoes and the white hair. She told me that she had done what the old Jewish saying advises: when faced with two choices, find a third. She had thought there were only two choices available to her after her husband's death: dying or taking care of yet another sick and careworn soul. She hadn't realized there was an alternative—to live her life purposefully in the time that was left—until she'd chosen it.

Telling the neighbors that another friend needed caring for, she set off for Sheep Mountain. Was lying necessary? This was the early 1970s, Nasim told me, and people in Wyoming were still living in the 1950s. She didn't want to be known as the town eccentric. Too exhausting a role. Besides, only southerners and the British could appreciate really good eccentrics.

She climbed Sheep Mountain. It took her from dawn to just before dusk, on a little trail carved by deer and sheep. Her chest hurt so badly that she feared a heart attack, but she reached the top and set up camp. First out of the pack were her field guides: one for flowers, one for birds, one for trees, one for mammals, one for stars. The tent was unwieldy and she settled for spreading the canvas out on the ground and unrolling her sleeping bag on top of it. Wrapped in an army blanket, she sat and listened to the wind as her tiny propane stove boiled water for tea. The wind seemed to come from all four directions in gusts.

In the Lakota tradition, she told me, the wind is divided into four. Four wind brothers blowing from the north, south, east, and west. A fifth wind brother moves about and has no fixed position. The north wind is icy, with a touch that can kill. The south wind is friendly. The east wind, slow and mean. The west, full of thunder and lightning.

In Latvian mythology, wind is not a brother, but a mother. When Latvians of centuries past felt the wind's cool touch as it swept across the Baltic Sea from Sweden, they knew that Veja Mate, Mother of Winds, had arrived. As Veja Mate caressed the forests with her long hands, the larch trees relaxed their rigid stance and swayed; and as she moved across the fields and meadows, she blew softly on her little silver whistle and the swallows flew up to meet her.

If the Latvians had known of atmospheric science, they would have created three mothers of the four winds: Mother Pressure, Mother Friction, and Mother Coriolis. Mother Pressure thickens and thins the air, and these differences in air pressure create the winds. The differences occur when some areas of the land warm up faster under the sun's touch than other areas. In a high-pressure area, falling air prevents the updrafts clouds need to birth rain showers. This is why a high-pressure area generally means clear weather. Air flows from the high-pressure area to low-pressure areas. When pressure differences equalize, the wind dies.

At the same time, another force is influencing the wind, and that is Mother Friction. The wind skates across the planet's surface, gathering speed where the surface is smoother, slowing down where it is rougher. Forests and cities create friction, slowing the wind down. Lakes and oceans, prairies and high plains create less friction and so the wind speeds up as it moves across those surfaces.

The third force acting on the wind is Mother Coriolis. Because the planet is spinning, the wind doesn't move in a straight line but curves instead. In the northern hemisphere, wind and water turn right in a clockwise direction. In the southern hemisphere, they curve to the left.

As I sit in the gray-green prickle of prairie northeast of town, a ferruginous hawk hangs motionless in the wind, while farther up cirrus clouds glide in the opposite direction. Now and then the wind brings the cries of gulls from the city dump several miles away, where the birds spiral endlessly above the ripening garbage. The winds are more complex than I had thought. They flow simultaneously at different altitudes, different speeds, and the three forces act on them at once. Meanwhile, the planet spins.

Nasim told me that when the men on horseback rode up the next morning to see who was on their land, her appearance came in handy. They let her stay, though she could hear them snickering as they rode away on their bay quarter horses with black roached manes. She knew they had labeled her according to their own lexicon, and it wasn't a particularly flattering one, but she didn't care. They had let her stay.

At night she could see the lights of Laramie like a spill of glittering broken glass. The isolated chips of light studding the valley floor were ranches. Red radio beacons blinked from the towers outside of town, regular in rhythm as a cow chewing its cud. To the south, west, and north, an occasional lonely light sparkled in the darkness. But above, the entire night sky and all the ancient stars looked upon her.

For the first time since she was a young girl she felt that thrill of excitement, she said. It was like standing at the end of a high diving board and looking out across a great blue pool. She felt truly alive at that moment, full of possibility.

Nasim tried to convey this feeling the last time I visited her house. She was planting white petunias and red geraniums in the front yard and I was helping her, as her hands had developed a tremor. I hadn't seen her in months; I'd met a boy and was swimming in the middle of a sixteen-year-old's pond of infatuation.

Over those months, she seemed to have aged drastically. As we knelt in the dirt, she coughed deeply. Her hands shook even when at rest. She moved with great care.

The wind ruffled the petals of the white petunias. Cotton floated down in the clumps from the great female cottonwoods around us, clinging to the red ball flowers and sticky green stems of pelargonium. A few sprinkles of rain came down as we finished, and the sky grumbled. We went inside. I was telling her about the boy—I could have talked for days about him—when she walked over to the refrigerator and took out what looked like some meat or bones wrapped in white butcher's paper. Suddenly, I saw the younger Nasim I had known as she thumped it down on the counter in front of me and ordered me to unwrap it.

"What is *that?*" I asked, looking with disgust at the gray and white and red mass on the paper in front of me.

"Cow's eye," she said briskly. "Got it at the meat packer's, down by the railroad yard."

"Good eating, huh? Do you bake it or fry it?" I giggled.

"I got it for *you,*" she said, pointing at me for emphasis. "There's something I remembered about cow's eyes that I wanted to show you."

She picked up a small, razor-blade-like knife and sliced without any tremor into the gray and red mass. I turned away in disgust but she put down the knife and grabbed my arm. "Just because something's unpleasant to you doesn't mean you have the right to look away," she said.

Frowning and inwardly protesting, I turned back and stood in front of the knot of flesh and sinew. She picked up the knife. "I know what you're thinking, honey, but open your mind. I know this animal was created to be meat for someone's table. But it breathed and ate and shivered and slept before it got there, and this eye looked upon the same mountains and sky that your eyes do, so have a little respect, young lady."

She cut some more. Then I saw it: the lump of gray and red was now recognizable as an eye. Her knife pried out a little round disc, an amber sliver, scratched and somewhat cloudy: the lens of the cow's eye. I shivered. She picked it up and placed it in the palm of my hand. Its hardness, somewhat like a piece of plastic, was as reassuring as the cool, dry scales of a snake's skin: that is, dreading to touch something slimy, one is relieved when it turns out to be dry and somewhat ordinary. This lens was merely one of the tools of life such as we all are given.

I'm sure she showed me the optic nerve and the cornea, but what I remember next is how her scalpel sliced the eyeball, round as a tangerine, in half. Two tiny bowls lay on the counter, formerly one eye. Inside was a lining of blue, electrifying in its richness, more beautiful than sapphire, cobalt, or lapis. That color leaps across the decades, burned on the retina of my mind. It is one shard of memory that still has the power to startle me. How could such a vibrant blue be hidden away in a globular gray mass like that? What purpose, this beauty?

Nasim put down the scalpel. I think she was satisfied.

SPECKLED RISING WIND

Summer

∾   A PHOTOGRAPH TAKEN in July over twenty-five years ago shows a brown child, my brother Mark, squatting in the red-brown dirt behind our house. His hands cradle a small green plant. Beside him fingers of leaf lettuce line up in rows and thin-armed bean plants grope skyward. Behind him a blur of white and pink sweetpeas climbs the chicken wire fence; the wind must have been blowing through them as their curling vines are smudged. Beyond the garden, if one could call that plot of wishful thinking a garden, stretches olive green prairie. My favorite place, the rock circle in the far hillside, appears as a half-moon of shadow while the twin bunkers of red dirt we scavenged daily for bones and china and lavender glass look distant and mysterious. To the south of that, Lamb's ranch is a line of dark fuzz where rising land becomes full-fledged foothill. A stark bluish white sky arching across to touch the gray-blue berm of the Laramie Mountains promises a hot day.

It's just a snapshot. Yet looking at it, I am struck by my ignorance in assuming none of that pictured world would change. Just because the sky was so huge and blue, and the land so sweeping and green, and the mountains so old and stable, with their comforting rounded shoulders, I thought everything would always be the same. But look at the snapshot for clues: behind our little garden and the bigger one of our Seventh Day Adventist neighbors, who lived off their produce all fall and winter, orange and yellow surveyor's stakes are stuck in the ground.

Nothing in that photograph would look the same the following summer: not the garden, not the prairie, not the ranch, not the boy. I clutch the photograph, my artifact, as one would an arrowhead or pottery shard or old lavender glass medicine bottle. It is all I have.

～ ～ ～

By the time I was seventeen that prairie was all plowed and flattened and homes and roads were cluttering its simple curves. Looking for a cause, or maybe a distraction, I found a summer job at a nursing home as a nurse's aide. My mother, a nurse, warned me that the job was messier than my idealism could handle. I ignored her.

Time crawled that summer as I became intimate with the side effects of old age in all its incontinent glory. I learned to wrap a blood-pressure cuff around a bony arm and listen for the pulse of a hard-worn heart. I learned to take a temperature and give a sponge bath. I learned how to move a man twice my weight and how to change a bed with a woman still in it. I liked the old cowboys—the red- and pink-skinned one named Bucky, and the walnut-skinned one named Lovey—and wished I had more time to listen to them when they were lucid. I liked some of the fine old women who held onto any shred of dignity they could —Helen and Mrs. G. But I disliked almost everyone else. I tried shamefully to pretend they weren't human or that they didn't exist at all as I fed them dinner or wiped their genitals.

One evening I was assigned to a new wing. We were pulling bodies into wheelchairs for the journey to the dining hall when I entered a room and found a woman huddled on her bed. Her white hair was a tangled bird's nest. Her arms were as thin as a crane's legs, and folded tightly against her chest. Her legs were folded too, bent at the knees, and as white as rice paper. She looked like a bird. Her face was turned toward the window and I couldn't tell if she was asleep or awake, alive or dead.

I walked around to the other side of the bed, then stopped. The eyes were closed, but that face— the nose sharper, the cheekbones more angular—it looked a thinner twin of an old, familiar face. But how could it be? I'd just seen her only a few months before. Or had it been a year? School and boyfriend had kept me busy and I hadn't had time to visit. No, it couldn't be her. She would have called me. Someone would have told me she was here.

"Hello? Can you hear me? It's dinner time," I said softly.

Her eyes opened. I gasped. It *was* her. But she was staring at the window, not even looking at me. The sky was clear and the pines near the nursing home wore the golden light of the summer evening.

I stepped closer to the bed. "Mrs. Sands— Nasim. It's me, Carol. Carol Jakubauskas. Do you remember me?"

Her eyes wrenched away from the window and bored into mine. She took a deep breath, as if surprised. Then she whispered hoarsely, "Get out."

I stared at her. "What do you mean? Don't you know who I am? I'm here to help you—"

"Get…out."

I froze. She tensed her whole body, arching her back as she took another breath. "Get out!" she cried. "Get out! Get out!"

I ran into the corridor. Another aide was wheeling an elderly woman who was helpfully pushing the wheelchair of an elderly man. Their little train stopped and all three looked over at me with great interest.

"Something wrong?" the aide asked.

"She started shouting at me. What do I do?"

"Sounds like one of her fits. She can be the biggest bitch for being so tiny. Go down to the station and tell the nurse. She'll give her some Darvon to calm down."

I ran down the hall to the nurses' station. "There's a problem in room four. Mrs. Sands—she's shouting. She needs help." I took my stethoscope out of my white coat pocket and placed it on the counter.

"Yes? So what's wrong?" The nurse didn't lift her head from her paperwork.

"She's screaming. Maybe she's in pain. She won't stop." I took the blood pressure cuff and bulb out of my pocket and laid them on the counter beside the stethoscope. Then I started to unbutton my white uniform.

The nurse looked up. "What are you doing?"

"I'm quitting." I laid the white coat on the counter. In my t-shirt and jeans I felt suddenly cold.

"You can't leave now, in the middle of the shift."

"I have to," I said, heading for the door. "Don't forget room four." I strode past room after room of huddled bodies and confused faces, gathering momentum as I went.

She caught up with me at the front door. "Just what the hell do you think you're doing?" she shouted.

"I can't stay here."

"If you walk out you'll never work here again!" she yelled. I opened the glass doors and felt the evening's fresh breath on my arms.

"That's the idea," I muttered, and began to run.

∾   ∾   ∾

I never saw Nasim again. I graduated from high school early and began attending classes at the University of Wyoming. When my parents moved to New York State, I elected to stay behind, along with my sister, who boarded with her best friend's family while finishing her senior year in high school. Immersed in my own little world of college classes, and later, in young married life, I turned away from my high school friends, old neighbors, and the people I knew from my mother's church. I rarely even saw my sister. At the time, I told myself that I was leaving the past and my childish ways behind, moving into adulthood and forging a new life for myself.

But I knew, underneath it all, I was wrong. Pretending I had no past was not the path to adulthood. I had abandoned Nasim and I was in the process of abandoning the rest of my childhood. A quiet voice inside me said I should have gone back to see her in the nursing home when I had the chance. Still, I was afraid to call the nursing home, afraid to call the newspaper and ask if they had published an obituary for her. Afraid, perhaps, that she was still alive and I would then have to go see her.

One snowy day two years later, as I was taking a shortcut across the cemetery near the university, I veered off the dirt road and stepped into the little cemetery office. I was very pregnant, and I needed a rest from the cold and wind before heading on to class. On impulse I asked the man in the office, where was Mrs. Sands' grave? Was there a grave for Mrs. Sands?

He checked his records, then pulled out a little map of the cemetery and pointed at the row. He circled two adjacent plots on the map. I walked along the dirt road, around one row of graves, then around another.

Soon I would be late for my exam. I hurried down another row. Why are you doing this? Leave it alone, a voice in my head said. Still I kept walking. Finally I found the headstones. They were unpolished, simple, carved of native rosy sandstone, the same material as Nasim's house. Her idea, I'm sure. I touched the letters and numbers signifying two lives begun and ended, two pixels in the enormous photograph of time. Then I ran to class, one hand beneath my heavy belly.

∾ ∾ ∾

After a while we notice the years of our lives accumulating like dried leaves piled in an untended garden. Or maybe a more apt metaphor—it's as if each of us stands on an ice floe, adrift in a great cold sea. Each year part of the ice floe is chipped away and disappears into the dark blue water. Then at age thirty-five or forty we suddenly realize that a larger portion of the floe has been chipped away than the remaining piece underfoot. The nearness of the cold water is shocking, as is the smallness of the ice floe that is left, and the speed with which it has disappeared.

I wish I could tell Nasim this and watch her snort in disbelief at how someone not yet forty could make such a big deal out of aging. "You think this is bad," she'd say, laughing. "You're in for a big surprise when you hit eighty, dear."

I thought of her as I went out recently, into the speckled rising wind, to revisit my old special place. Yes, I had found it, and had almost wished I hadn't, but still, I wanted to see it again. Nasim had been there once, after I'd asked her to look at it and tell me exactly what the rock circle had been—a quarry? A meteor crater? An ancient seashore? She sat on the ledge and touched the rock wall but gave me no answer.

Once again, driving north, then east, north, then east, I found the farthest northeast street and parked my car. Nervously I got out. The small, cheap aluminum windows of the houses seemed to watch me.

I walked across a scraped-off lot, then around two piles of leftover rock and past a freshly poured concrete foundation. I half expected someone to come out of one of the nearby houses and demand that I get off the land. However, no one stopped me. Maybe it was the camera and notepad I carried, hoping I'd look like a scientist or a student, as if that gave me a greater right to be there. More likely it was that no one in these houses ever needed to look outside. Why bother? All they would see were more houses. *And* a little piece of prairie.

I clambered over more piles of dumped stones, plywood scrap, concrete droppings, until finally my feet touched prairie again. The curly grasses crunched beneath my boots and I smelled the sharp odor of sage-brush. Here and there, between patches of ground cover and buffalo grass, I saw Earth's skin, red dirt and pale yellow rock. As I walked I counted wildflowers blooming. Ten kinds. And there, suddenly, it was: the rock circle.

Only part of it had been filled in with leftover construction debris. I could still make out the old rock walls, only three feet high by my guess, set into the hillside. I'd thought they were higher. And there were the ledges where my dog and I would sit and gaze down valley at the town, miles away. Only now the town was a couple of hundred feet away and the dog was dead. I stood for a while on a ledge, listening, waiting, then hiked up the hill behind the rock circle. Rough stones big as fists clinked beneath my boots sounding like fired porcelain pots knocking against each other. Dry and brittle, they were colored in hues I'd forgotten: orange, pale rust, bone, ash, grayish pink, lavender. Picking pieces of them up, I felt I was gathering teeth or bones from a shattered corpse. Bright orange circles of lichen were splashed on some of the rocks, as if on a particularly amazing day eons ago, orange rain had fallen.

My special place had survived, just barely.

The wind stilled. From the hilltop I heard a carillon of bells from town. The caw of a crow.

Whistles of sparrows, a handful of them flung out from the sagebrush near my boots. No meadowlarks. They were probably the first to leave after the bulldozers came.

I walked as an adult walks, bowed, heavy-shouldered. My brain remembered another way of walking, lighter, full of grace, but my body could not reproduce it. My boots crushed a spray of sagebrush and I inhaled my past, realizing that the reason for my sluggishness was that I was looking for something. Looking for a sign. I was hoping, I admit, to find some evidence of my younger self and her dog. Perhaps a word or initials scratched in a rock, or a hat forgotten under a sagebrush bush, or maybe a more subtle trace than that.

But as it is with all gradual leave-takings, the thought had never occurred to me that I'd ever be separated from this place. So I had left no signs and now I found no signs of myself, nor the dog, nor my brother. Three rusted cans of indeterminate age. We wouldn't have left them out there, my later sofa-dumping notwithstanding. Two pillows, recently forgotten, probably brought out by children from these nearby houses. Bits of cardboard. Shards of crockery with old white crackle glaze. A piece of brown glass from a beer bottle. Nothing to say I'd even passed through there. Silently I walked back to my car. Then I realized something—this was how it was supposed to be.

The land had never needed me. I was nothing to it. I moved across it like a cloud shadow, and when I left, nothing grieved. I had mourned the loss of the prairie, cleared off and flattened, scores of streets carved in the dirt and lined with house after banal house. I had longed for that paradise of unchangingness that exists only in the human imagination. But only the land was meant to last, in whatever incarnation. Only the land and the wind.

I had been privileged to roam this place and learn without knowing I was learning. I knew how the wind felt at noon blowing hot and pungent among the sagebrush and how far it could carry the grasshoppers on summer mornings and how quickly it could scour the snow off the buffalo grass on winter afternoons. I knew how it felt to run jackrabbit-fast, with an Australian sheepdog by my side, as the setting sun painted the land in glowing rose and gold and stretched our shadows much bigger than we'd ever become. I had been privileged and not known it.

Recently Nasim's neighbor died. Among his things his daughter came across a little oil painting that Nasim had given him and she offered it to me. It was painted as if once at sunset, Nasim had been out there with us, amidst bunchgrass and sagebrush. In her narrow, bird-foot handwriting, in pencil at the bottom, are the words "Child and Dog Running Across Prairie, 1974." The girl, tall and gangly, her mouth open in laughter, flies across the wind-whipped buffalo grass with the small black dog loping beside her. Ahead of them lies more prairie and eternal sunlight, and at their heels, though it cannot be seen, the wind follows, always the wind. They run there forever.

To love the land was all.

Caroline Marwitz is an assistant professor at Regis University in Denver, Colorado. She lives with her husband and three sons in Denver and is currently finishing her first novel, *Chameleon Man,* and beginning work on her second book of nonfiction, *Eye.*